Mouse Ears for Everyone!

A Guide to Walt Disney World for Guests with Special Needs

2018 EDITION

Amy Schinner

Theme Park Press
www.ThemeParkPress.com

Editor: Bob McLain
Layout: Artisanal Text
Cover Design: Nathan Elsener

ISBN 978-1-68390-049-8
Printed in the United States of America

Theme Park Press | www.ThemeParkPress.com
Address queries to bob@themeparkpress.com

Contents

Introduction

Crowds, new schedules, heat, fireworks...these words are often associated with Walt Disney World (WDW) and other vacations and do not sound like a good fit to many families. How could this possibly be a good idea? Vacations are an important part of family bonding and growing up. The experiences I had on vacation helped me create memories with my family that have lasted a lifetime.

For example, even as adults we giggle over the time my sister, Emily, threw up on our grandma in the car. We had to stop at a waterfall to clean up Grandma and the car as best as we could. Naturally, by "we" I mean our parents, while Emily, our brother Nathan, and I played at the waterfall. This was not a picture-perfect vacation moment planned by my parents, but it became a part of the experience that has remained with us forever.

The great thing about reading a book is you can use as much or as little of it as you want. The same is true of the advice given. Every family needs to do things that work for them. I believe if you even picked this book up to look at it you must have an interest. That being said, I understand that Walt Disney World doesn't work for everyone. This book will give you the best information I have for making a WDW vacation successful, or maybe enough to learn that it still isn't a good fit. Your family might be better suited for a trip to the Great Smoky Mountains or any number of other cool places.

My first passion is helping families; my excitement for Disney and all it can offer is second. I hope you see the possibilities about travel and have a magical time with your family.

Before You Leave Home

Is Disney the Right Fit?

The Disney company is the world's gold standard for customer service. Their mission is to ensure that guests have the most magical experience possible. Millions of people visit Walt Disney World every year from all over the world. The needs of each guest vary, with some having needs greater than most. Since 1971, Disney cast members have been helping to make guests with disabilities comfortable at their resort. These decades of experience allow families to enjoy the parks with as little complication as possible.

In addition to Disney's guest services, Disney magic shouldn't be overlooked. No, not actual hocus-pocus, but there is something real about being surrounded by the music, characters, and stories we love. For example, I was very nervous about our first trip with my son, Ben, when he was three. He is on the autism spectrum and we just didn't know how he would react. Magic! He greeted characters, he smiled constantly, and opened up more. To this day, the only explanation I have is that surrounding him with things he enjoyed allowed him to relax a little.

As you can see, with a combination of world-class service and some pixie dust, a Disney vacation can be the right fit for every family.

Who Is This Book Written For?

One evening at Barnes and Noble, a frequent night out for my family, I was looking at the travel section and noticed the many travel guides for Walt Disney World. My family has been traveling to WDW for years, so I never really looked closely at the guidebooks before. There were guides for so many "categories," such as kids, dining, and those on a budget, but nothing for families and individuals with special needs. That led me to check out the special needs and parenting sections...still nothing.

I answer questions for families all the time about how we do WDW with Ben, so next thing I knew, I started writing this book.

Mouse Ears for Everyone is for any family that is living with a disability. Mobility issues are a challenge at WDW, but so is autism, anxiety, developmental disabilities, food allergies, and eating challenges. The goal was to create a book that will help families find answers to their questions and assist them in planning a magical Disney vacation.

How to Use This Book

Mouse Ears for Everyone has three sections. The first section contains information on planning a Disney vacation. The second section focuses on navigating the parks. The third section includes information on some of the attractions outside of the park, such as Disney Springs, the water parks, and mini golf.

There are many acronyms and special terms that are specific to the disability community, and to the Disney parks and resorts. Here are some of the more common ones you'll encounter in this book:

Disability Terms

Accessible
Safe for any mobility equipment

ADA
American Disabilities Act

ASD
Autism-Spectrum Disorder (autism)

Non-physical disability
Any disability without a physical impairment

Non-visible disability
Any disability without a physical characteristic

Typically developing (neuro-typical)
A child without a developmental disability

Sensory spot
A spot or attraction that is good for a little escape

Sensory Impact
How loud or disconcerting something is

Headphones
Noise-reducing headphones

Transfer
An attraction that requires you to move out of your wheelchair onto the ride.

Frontloading
Preparing and talking about what will be happening

Mobility issue
Disabilities that make it hard or impossible to walk, or even to move

Standard wheelchair
Not a cart or ECV, and sometimes not even a rental wheelchair

Mobility Chair
A larger mobile chair like a stroller needed for mobility and other needs

Stroller as a Wheelchair
A traditional stroller needed for a child with a disability and has a pass from Disney with this designation

ECV
An electric cart used like a wheelchair

Disney Terms

Cast member
Any Disney employee

Backstage
Any area not open to the public

On stage
Any area open to the public

Rope drop
Being at a park just before opening

Guest
Visitor or customer

FastPass+
A reservation made to enter a ride or show that cuts down on wait times

MyDisneyExperience
An app that allows you to make FastPasses, shows wait times, and is your digital guide to Walt Disney World

Magic Hours
When the park is open for resort guests only

Stroller parking
An area to park strollers because they aren't allowed on a ride or at a show

DAS (Disability Access Service)
The reservation system used for wait times if you need accommodations due to a non-visible disability

The recommendations in this book consider the needs of families and guests with disabilities for every attraction, every hotel, and many of the restaurants. I am not a food or travel critic. I will simply let you know what is available, the price point, and make recommendations based on accessibility, sensory impact, and personal experience.

Why Is All of This Necessary?

I know this is a lot of information—after all it's a whole book! You may be like my sister and think, 'Why can't I just book a room and show up?' Technically, you can, but let's be honest: traveling to Disney is a major financial investment, so you'll want to make sure you are getting your money's worth. If you don't have a plan, you spend a lot of time in lines and waste precious hours trying to figure out the best places to be for your family.

I realize there are more reservations involved in a Disney vacation than for most other destinations, but let's all remember, with family members that require more assistance, or a specific schedule, there is more planning to go anywhere, every day.

An Overview of Walt Disney World

With 27,258 acres of land, Walt Disney World can best be described as HUGE. There are 4 theme parks, 27 Disney Resort hotels, 9 hotels that aren't run by Disney (including the military hotel Shades of Green), 2 water parks, 4 golf courses, a shopping and entertainment district, a complete sports complex, and so much more. Because of its size, very little at the resort is a "quick walk" away.

The four major theme parks will be your main focus:

- The Magic Kingdom is the crown jewel of Walt Disney World. It's where the iconic attractions such as Cinderella Castle, Haunted Mansion, and Pirates of the Caribbean are located.
- Epcot is two parks in one: Future World and World Showcase. The landmark is a giant "golf ball" named Spaceship Earth.
- Disney's Hollywood Studios places you in the heart of Old Hollywood.
- Disney's Animal Kingdom is a combination of thrill rides, shows, and a spectacular opportunities for animal observation and interaction.

The resort hotels are spread throughout the property, with many options available in terms of location, theming, and price.

Disney Springs (formally Downtown Disney) is a shopping and entertainment complex featuring a movie theater, Disney-themed and high-end shopping, Disney Quest (a large arcade with virtual attractions), a bowling alley, and restaurants.

In addition to the parks, resorts, and Disney Springs, there are water parks, golf and mini-golf, boat rides, and even horseback riding and archery. There is no way to do it all during one vacation. Therefore, the goal of this book is to help you figure out what your family wants to see and what special needs must be considered, and then and how to manage all of that in order to have a successful vacation.

SECTION ONE

On Your Mark

Planning and Prepping for Your Vacation

CHAPTER ONE

When to Go

I hate to say it, but there really is no magic bullet for this one. There are many charts that calculate crowd levels, weather, etc., but families have many things that can direct when they are able to get away. Some of them are typical, like school and work, but sometimes the special needs a family member has to work with, like heat sensitivities or treatment schedules, dictate their calendar. Even family plans such as reunions or weddings at Disney World can decide for you. The good news is that whenever you go, policies are in place to help you have a magical time.

Crowds

Crowd levels at WDW don't just affect lines for rides, they affect everything—food lines, traffic, bus lines, parking—and at times there are literally wall to wall people, with little room to move. There are policies to help alleviate some of that, but you will still have more to deal with as the crowd levels increase.

The rule of thumb is when school is out the parks are more crowded. Summer and holidays allow more families to travel; therefore, everything takes a little (or a lot) longer. The natural conclusion to that would be if you are able, go during school, but that can have its downsides as well.

In this chapter I've broken down the pros and cons of each month:

January

- *Crowd*: low
- *Budget*: better deals can be found
- *Weather*: cool
- *Events*: marathon, Martin Luther King weekend, Epcot International Festival of the Arts
- *Maintenance*: likely
- *Weird notables*: the crane is up behind the castle; it will be in pictures

February

- *Crowd*: low
- *Budget*: better deals can be found
- *Weather*: cool
- *Events*: Presidents' Day, Epcot International Festival of the Art
- *Maintenance*: likely

March

- *Crowd*: picking up for spring break (if Easter is in March, the weeks before and after are high)
- *Budget*: regular to high (based on holiday)
- *Weather*: warmer but not high humidity
- *Events*: Epcot International Flower and Garden Show, Atlanta Braves at ESPN Wide World of Sports Complex for spring break (final season at WDW is 2018)
- *Maintenance*: usually light

April

- *Crowd*: picking up for spring break
- *Budget*: regular to high (based on holiday)
- *Weather*: warmer but not high humidity (brave souls call it pool weather)
- *Events*: Epcot International Flower and Garden Show, spring break
- *Maintenance*: usually light

May

- *Crowd*: light
- *Budget*: regular
- *Weather*: warmer but not high humidity
- *Events*: Epcot International Flower and Garden Show, Memorial Day
- *Maintenance*: usually light

June

- *Crowd*: regular to higher
- *Budget*: regular to high (there are usually deals for early June)
- *Weather*: summer
- *Events*: school is out; if you are an area that gets out of school early, don't wait for the end of the month

July

- *Crowd*: high and very high during the holiday week
- *Budget*: holiday high to regular high
- *Weather*: summer
- *Events*: Fourth of July
- *Maintenance*: usually light

August

- *Crowd*: regular to higher (Labor Day)
- *Budget*: regular to lower; there are deals to be found as school resumes
- *Weather*: summer, hurricane season
- *Events*: Labor Day, some schools back in session, Mickey's Not-So-Scary Halloween Party
- *Maintenance*: usually light

September

- *Crowd*: regular to lower
- *Budget*: regular to lower (there are deals); check for free Disney dining
- *Weather*: still warm or even hot, hurricane season
- *Events*: Mickey's Not So Scary Halloween Party, Epcot Food and Wine Festival
- *Maintenance*: more attractions are closed for repairs
- *Note*: If you have a child who does not enjoy Halloween, then no matter how family friendly it is (and of course it is!), I would *not* recommend September for your family. Why make them uneasy?

October

- *Crowd*: regular
- *Budget*: regular
- *Weather*: still warm, hurricane season
- *Events*: Mickey's Not So Scary Halloween Party, Epcot Food and Wine Festival
- *Maintenance*: more attractions are closed for repair.
- *Weird notables*: the crane is up behind the castle, it will be in pictures.
- *Note*: If you have a child who does not enjoy Halloween, then no matter how family friendly it is (and of course it is!), I would *not* recommend September for your family. Why make them uneasy?

November

- *Crowd*: light (except for Thanksgiving week)
- *Budget*: regular (except for Thanksgiving week)
- *Weather*: still warm, less chance but still hurricane season
- *Events*: Mickey's Very Merry Christmas Party, Epcot Food and Wine Festival, Epcot's International Festival of the Holidays (11/19)
- *Maintenance*: closer to the end of the month most rides are open.
- *Note*: Holiday decorations start going up on the November 1, but if you want to see all of them, plan for closer to Thanksgiving.

December

- *Crowd*: regular to crazy high
- *Budget*: high
- *Weather*: still warm with cool nights
- *Events*: Mickey's Very Merry Christmas Party, Epcot's International Festival of the Holidays, Christmas Tree Walk, New Years Eve, special parades, fireworks, decorations, and celebrations in all four parks and Disney Springs
- *Maintenance*: most everything is open
- *Note*: I don't recommend going the week before or after Christmas. The crowds are at the highest levels, and most days the Magic Kingdom is at capacity, which means you can enter only if you are a park guest. However, the first two weeks of December have a little extra pixie dust if you can arrange it.

Weather Patterns

If your vision of a Florida vacation includes shorts and pool time, do not travel during the winter months; it gets cooler than you might think.

On the other hand, if the idea of the heat and humidity is not appealing at all, then you should really enjoy Orlando's mild weather October through April.

If you are concerned about weather extremes on either side of the spectrum, I would suggest the first two weeks of May (so you miss the spring break crowds) or October and November.

Average temperatures and rainfall in Orlando, Florida (from noaa.com):

Month	High	Low	Rain
January	71.8°	49.9°	2.43"
February	73.9°	51.3°	2.35"

March	78.8°	55.9°	3.54”
April	83.0°	59.9°	2.42”
May	88.2°	65.9°	3.74”
June	91.0°	71.3°	7.35”
July	92.2°	72.6°	7.15”
August	92.0°	73.0°	6.25”
September	90.3°	71.9°	5.76”
October	85.0°	66.5°	2.73”
November	78.9°	58.7°	2.32”
December	73.3°	52.6°	2.31”

Do Days of the Week Matter?

Some experts claim to know the best days of the week to visit, but making these predictions is a crapshoot, and in any case, you sometimes can't fine-tune your vacation to take advantage of what parks might be marginally better choices on certain days of the week. Here are some rules of thumb:

- First-timers should always start at Magic Kingdom. If you don't, the kids will keep looking for it. They'll complain as they look for castles that aren't there, and so they won't fully experience what the other three parks have to offer.
- My family is able to get up early, so we enjoy morning magic hours. If you can do it, you get a lot of the parks accomplished in that time; then, if it's busier because everyone chose that park, go to a different one (if you have Park Hopper passes).
- I also think ending your trip at the Magic Kingdom (even if just for the evening) is the most magical and memorable finale for the vacation. Yes, my eyes mist up every time.

How Long Should We Stay?

Walt Disney World is huge. There is no way to see all of it in one vacation, but with a little time and planning, you can see everything that you want to.

There are a few things to consider in deciding how long you can stay:

- *Travel time.* How much of the time you can be away will be spent traveling? My family drives two days each way.
- *Budget.* Remember that there are daily expenses on top of lodging and tickets. Food, souvenirs, stroller or chair rentals, and incidentals add up quickly, plus there are usually unplanned expenses (like the Crocs we had to buy on our last trip because of blisters).

- *How much do you want to see?* Not everyone wants to see all four parks.

If you want to visit all four parks, I would recommend at least four days, even if you have Park Hoppers. Five or more days makes taking naps and breaks easier, and it allows for a more relaxing vacation.

Special Events

Special events occur throughout the year. Some of them might affect your decisions in picking a date.

Disney's Marathon. First weekend of the month (after New Year's). There are tens of thousands of runners that invade Walt Disney World for the marathon. Many of the locals even stay the night in a resort because it gives them easier access to the starting line.

Epcot International Festival of the Arts. January/February. Adding even more culture to the World Showcase is a festival celebrating art. Become a part of a famous painting, help create a mural, watch Broadway performers, take classes, and more. Then have a creative treat in one of the kiosks with art-themed treats.

NFL All-Star Game. January. The All Star Game has moved to Orlando with a multi-year agreement. The first year of that agreement is 2017, so the affect on crowd levels is unknown.

Atlanta Braves Spring Training. February and March. The Braves bring Major League Baseball to Disney World. After the 2018 season the Braves will be moving their team to a different stadium.

Epcot International Flower and Garden Show. March through May. I love this show. Epcot is at its most beautiful with the stunning flowers and topiaries. There are also food kiosks for additional small bites to eat and playgrounds that provide more sensory spots. I think this is the best time of the year for Epcot.

Mickey's Not So Scary Halloween Party. Certain dates in August, September, and October. This is a "hard-ticket event," which means the park closes at 7pm to guests with regular admission tickets and only guests that bought MNSSHP tickets are allowed to stay.

MNSSHP is a fun event party that allows guests of all ages to dress in (appropriate) costumes, trick or treat, enjoy themed parades, and fireworks and entertainment. Tickets are limited, so crowd size is reasonable.

If you have a ticket, you may enter Magic Kingdom at 4:00pm (or stay after 4:00pm if you're already there) and remain until close (it will be late). Some families choose to rest at the pool, miniature golf , resort hop, or do other activities during the day, and not use a regular park ticket from your package, then enjoy the party that evening. Other families choose to be at another park for that evening and not spend more on special tickets.

The theme for this party is of course Halloween. It is very tame as far as Halloween goes, but there is a focus on the villains, people are in costume, and the parade opens with a headless horseman riding down the street. If you are traveling with someone who won't like this, it's probably not a good fit.

Epcot Food and Wine Festival. September through mid-November. Epcot already has a diverse selection of restaurants in the World Showcase, but during the Food and Wine Festival there are booths and kiosks that make it practically explode with options.

I wish this festival also had the playgrounds like the Flower and Garden Show, but you eat standing up, and there aren't any specific kid activities beyond what Epcot already offers. I'm not sure I would make the trip specifically for this event, but it isn't a reason to avoid this time period either.

Mickey's Very Merry Christmas Party. Certain dates in November and December. This is a "hard-ticket event," which means the park closes at 7pm to guests with regular admission tickets and only guests who bought MVMCP tickets are allowed to stay.

Christmas comes alive at this fun party with specially themed parades, fireworks, and entertainment. It snows on Main Street and there are free cookies and cocoa (some years there have been waffles, too). Tickets are limited, so crowd size is reasonable.

If you have a ticket, you may enter Magic Kingdom at 4:00pm (or stay after 4:00pm if you're already there) and remain until close (it will be late). Some families choose to rest at the pool, miniature golf , resort hop, or do other activities during the day, and not use a regular park ticket from your package, then enjoy the party that evening. Other families choose to be at another park for that evening and not spend more on special tickets.

MVMCP is a *Christmas* party. There is no diversity in celebrations for this event.

.***Epcot International Festival of the Holidays.*** December. Epcot's World Showcase is decorated for the holidays just like the home countries would look. There are storytellers and different versions of Santa (Father Christmas) that bring the holidays to life. In the American Pavilion, there are stories about Hanukkah and Kwanza as well as Mr. and Mrs. Claus, the pavilions for Japan and China celebrate traditions from their culture including the Lunar New Year. New for 2017 is a scavenger hunt helping Chip and Dale find all of their ornaments, some tasty new food options, and a holiday finale for Illuminations.

CHAPTER TWO

It Always Comes Down to the Budget

There are so many ways to set a budget for a trip and you don't need me to do that for you. Also, since each family is different, not every upgrade or added activity that Disney offers will have equal appeal. Here are a few things to consider, bearing in mind your budget, length of stay, and family preference:

Tickets

Disney has several choices for tickets:

- *One-Day, One-Park Pass.* You can visit one park only that day. You may leave and come back to that park, but no other park.
- *One-Day Park Hopper.* You may visit all four parks on your single day.
- *Multi-Day Pass.* This pass allows you to go to one park a day for however many days you paid for. Example: Monday, Magic Kingdom; Tuesday, Epcot; Wednesday, Magic Kingdom; etc. You may visit any of the four main parks, but only the same park each day, for example, morning at Animal Kingdom, back to the room to break, back to Animal Kingdom.
- *Multi Day with Park Hopper.* You may go to any of the four main parks any time you like for as many days as you purchased. Example: Monday morning, Magic Kingdom, then Disney's Hollywood Studios; Tuesday, Epcot, then Animal Kingdom; etc.
- *Multi Day with Park Hopper and More.* Like the multi-day Park Hoppers, but they include water parks and other activities.

I highly suggest upgrading to the Park Hopper. When we go, my family likes to break it up, but the biggest reason for the Park Hopper is being able to go back to visit favorite rides. If you are traveling with someone with a developmental disability, they can easily fixate on a certain ride. My son loves Toy Story Mania at Disney's Hollywood Studios. He needs to be able to get back to that ride in order to enjoy the rest of the vacation. If you can only do one park a day, it greatly affects your flexibility.

If you do not plan on going to the water parks, I do not recommend the "and More" option.

Lodging

There are a few things to upgrade here. My first suggestion is to stay in the parks. Convenience is the most important factor; it is easier to navigate and plan if everything is on resort property, plus you are able to book FastPasses and dinner reservations earlier than guests that stay off property.

My second housing upgrade recommendation is staying in a moderate resort or higher. The value resorts can seem like a great option, and they are if you need them to stay within your budget, but if you can swing the Caribbean Beach or another moderate or even better a deluxe, it is worth it.

There are a couple reasons for this recommendation. Space: the value rooms are pretty tight, and if you are adding medical or mobility equipment, they are especially tight. Noise is also a factor. The value rooms have very thin walls. I'm not exaggerating when I say I could hear every word from my neighbors and I could hear them in the bathroom. Add to that the groups of dancers and teams of soccer players, cheerleaders, and many other school groups, and there is a lot of activity that would be nice to avoid.

Another important consideration for staying on property is accessible transportation. The Disney buses and two of the Minnie vans (a $20 shuttle service) are all capable of transporting wheelchairs, ECVs, and fold-up wheelchairs. The hotel shuttles on International Drive and other off-property hotels do not accommodate any mobility device other than electric wheelchairs.

Character Meals

If you are able to have one or two character meals, it is a really nice way to see characters and enjoy a nice mealtime with your family. There are character meals in every park, and some of the resorts as well. Character meals are worth the added investment for a few reasons:

- The characters come to you. You don't wait in line to see them; while your family is enjoying a meal, they come around to you.
- The pressure is off. If someone in your family has a hard time approaching a character, they don't have to in this setting. The characters come to you, and even if you don't want to get up, they will stand behind you for a picture. I have seen amazing interactions between kids and characters at these meals due to the lack of pressure.

- The siblings can meet and greet without bothering the guest that doesn't care to be that close to a character. If you have a little one that is very excited to meet Minnie Mouse, but their sibling is unsure, the characters pick up on that and will wave from afar, or ignore them if they are asked to do so.
- It's nice to just sit and eat sometimes. As busy as we are on vacation, it's great not to have to look for a table, and just enjoy the air-conditioning (or heat) along with some Disney magic.

Dessert Parties

Dessert parties are a reserved spot for events like parades, fireworks, and shows. They also include food and drink to help you justify the cost. For a family with special needs, I do recommend these parties if you can afford it. They are not necessary, but they make things a little easier, in several ways:

- You don't have to stake out a spot and wait an hour or more in crowds for an event to begin.
- You aren't crammed in with wall to wall people.
- There is room to wander and no need to be still.
- Some very nice food and beverages, mostly dessert, but a few appetizers, too. At the parties in Hollywood Studios and Epcot, there is usually alcohol as well (not at Magic Kingdom).
- There is a special platter filled with treats to accommodate a food allergy. Just be sure to let them know when you book the reservation and when you arrive.
- If you need to choose just one, I recommend Happily Ever After at the Magic Kingdom. This show has the most congestion and therefore the highest reward (even without the alchohol).

Minnie Vans

In Disney's version of Uber, a red van with white dots, comes and picks you up and will take you anywhere on property. The fee is $20 a ride (for the whole family, not per person) there is no tipping. Car seats and wheelchair lifts or ramps are available, and the drivers are Disney cast members.

If this is an upgrade that appeals to you, just go to your hotel's front desk and they will set you up.

Note: The service uses an app serviced by Lyft. You must have a smart phone and be comfortable using your credit card on it to use this service.

Disney Dining Plan

The Disney Dining Plan comes up as you book your vacation. You are asked on the phone or online if you would like to add it to your package. They tell you it means discounted dining during your stay. Yes, what they offer is discounted, but for many families it is still more than you would normally spend, because many families simply don't eat as much food as the plans allow. My family doesn't eat dessert at every meal, nor do each of us need appetizers at dinner. However, if your family has big eaters, it is great to have dinners already paid for before you even get to Florida.

If you want to have character meals every day, it might also be easier on the budget. Just be prepared for tipping as an extra for each meal. It adds up pretty quickly.

Note: In the spring and fall there are sometimes specials that include the dining plan for free, with a full-price room package. Do the math and make sure the dining plan is worth a full-price room.

Tours and Tea Parties

Tours and tea parties look like a lot of fun. There are several I would like to do, but they are truly extras. They don't help make your vacation easier, they are simply extras that can be very cool. The great news is your family won't even know they are happening. If you don't book any of these extras, like the Dolphin Experience or the tea party with Alice at the Grand Floridian, or a fireworks cruise, nobody will ever feel like they missed out.

PhotoPass / MemoryMaker

Memory Maker is a service that gives you all of the photos a Disney cast member takes during your vacation. There are photographers at character meet and greets, iconic photo spots, and on many of the rides. If you want this service, order it online before your vacation. If you wait until you get there, the price goes up. A few things to know: you can order just a few pictures, photographers will happily take pictures with your camera, and you have 30 days after your vacation to download all of the photos.

Ways to Save

If you take advantage of Disney's upgrades, you may need to save money elsewhere to afford them. Here are some of my favorite ways to do so:

- If you don't mind having a credit card, the Chase Visa Disney credit card provides discounts on merchandise, select dining, and there are special character meet and greets for card holders.

- You can pay for everything with Disney gift cards. For big items like your hotel or tickets, it will take a little time to enter each card, but at Sam's and Costco you can buy Disney gift cards in bulk at a discount. I have also purchased gift cards at my grocery store for gas points.
- Gift cards can be a great way to "pre-purchase" meals and souvenirs. We still charge to our room on our MagicBands, then each day pay it off with the gift card at the help desk in the hotel.
- Disney does run specials, like discounted rooms, extra days on your tickets, and free dining. Keep an eye out for them.
- Bring some snacks and breakfast foods with you. This is easiest when you drive, but other options include packing a suitcase with food (you'll need to check it, but even that fee can save money). Have food delivered to your room. The Green Grocer and other companies in Orlando offer a delivery service to the resorts.

Budgets are tricky; do what is best for your family. Our family focuses our budget on making our trip as comfortable as possible, when we can.

CHAPTER THREE

How to Get There

Since reality hasn't caught up with *Star Trek*, we still have to fly or drive to Walt Disney World. (There's also the train, but that's a very limited option to families in certain parts of the country.)

For many families this is the scariest part. Transportation. has many variables, and in some cases we can't really control our situation. Here are tips for making each way easier:

- Relax! This is all part of the journey. It will all be great, and any bumps in the road add to the story telling. If you are relaxed and happy, the rest of your family will sense that.
- Pack snacks. Having snacks your family loves will help in tricky situations. You can't have too much (unless they go over the liquid limit on airplanes.
- Did I mention headphones?
- Have chargers for the technology handy.
- Have little surprises ready, like new books or toys. Then, when traffic jams or flight delays happen, the focus will be on fun things.

Flying

Some families just live too far to drive. Flying is great, and it gets you there faster, but it requires more careful packing, and being familiar with the airport and airline policies. Some tips for flying:

- Get there early. It's always better early than late, and there are a lot of fun things to see in an airport to pass the time.
- Noise-reducing headphones.
- If a direct flight is available, take it. Fewer flights usually mean fewer complications.
- When you get to your gate, request early boarding if you want it. If you would like your family to run around until the last second, hold back to the end of the line.

- After you have booked your flight, contact the airline to request a caregiver seat. They are not allowed to charge you to put a caregiver with a passenger who has special needs. They may not seat a whole family together for no charge, but they will make sure your passenger with a disability isn't alone. The bigger airlines make this very simple; the discount airlines push back, but don't back down.
- Make an appointment with TSA to arrange for help going through security. Call 855 787-2227 and the representatives will have you all set up. This makes a big difference in lines and patience shown in getting everyone through the lines. Although it is more comfortable for those with special needs, it might not be the faster route.
- If you don't feel the need for extra help, be prepared to let the agents know they are dealing with a non-visible disability, andthey will be more understanding. My son, Ben, does really well, but as an agent was barking orders, I simply said "autism" and he understood.
- Keep all medications and medical supplies in your carry-on. Check with TSA online to see how to pack needles if necessary.
- Remember, passengers under 10 years old and over 70 do not have to take off their shoes.
- Unfortunately, wheelchairs and strollers do need to be closely inspected. TSA will require most children to get out of strollers (even if they are sleeping) and a pat down will be required.
- Remember the liquid rules. When you are packing snacks, things like applesauce are considered a liquid. Have them in a quart-size Ziploc bag. Have empty cups, then once you are past security, fill them with drinks you purchase in the terminal. Formula is an exception, but read the websites for the current rules.
- Take everyone to the bathroom close to boarding time. The Orlando International Airport (MCO) has four bathrooms with adult-sized changing tables. There is one in each terminal.

The web site friendshipcircle.org has a great explanation of passenger rights and what to expect.

Flying with a Service Animal. The Air Carrier Access Act allows service and emotional support animals to fly free of charge on all airlines flying in the United States. There are, however, some requirements that you will need to be aware of to make your experience as smooth as possible.

- Have the required identification and papers.

- Service dogs should be in a solid-colored vest with patches to identify them. You'll need the dog's photo ID from an agency like the National Service Animal Registry.
- Emotional support animals will require a letter from a mental health professional. Some airlines require a form of their own be filled out by your doctor or counselor.
- After your tickets have been purchased, call the airline's accessibility number. Most airlines require at least 48 hours notice when traveling with a service or emotional support animal.
- Therapy animals that come to hospitals and nursing homes are not included in the Air Carrier Access Act. They are not allowed to travel with you for free.

Now that you have prepared the airline for your arrival, what do you do when you get to the airport?

- Visit the airline desk. As they load your baggage and give you a boarding pass, tell them you are traveling with a service or emotional support animal.
- They will ask for documentation (so many people try to fake an emotional support animal now that they will certainly ask for papers).
- You may carry your animal through the scanner, but remember to take off the collar, leash, and anything with metal.
- After security, proceed to your gate. Check in at the desk and inform them you are traveling with a service dog or emotional support animal.
- If they don't offer, ask for early entry; that will help give you more room to have everything and everyone in their places.
- Animals are not allowed to be in the aisle at all, and most airline attendants will ask you to have your animal on the floor behind the seat in front of you.

Tips for flying with an animal:

- Limit water intake.
- Try for direct flights.
- If you have to leave a secure area for the animal to relieve itself, you must go back through security. Try to plan ahead. Apps such as "Working Like a Dog" list airport relief areas.

Flying with a Wheelchair. If you're wheelchair-bound, or will need a wheelchair or other mobility device at the airport, I suggest:

- A week before your flight, contact the airline to inform them of the accommodations you will need.
- Security will ask if you are mobile. If so, you will be asked to step out of the chair and go through the scanner then return to your chair on the other side. If you aren't, they will do a personal search of you and your chair.
- When you get to your gate, check in and let the attendant know if you need assistance getting to your seat. There are narrow chairs designed for planes.
- You will board the plane first, and they will safely store your chair. After landing, you will be the last to depart so flight attendants can assist you.
- If it's hard for you to walk long distances and you'll need to rent a wheelchair at the airport, research in advance the airport's skycap policy and the assistance they offer. Call your airport and MCO (Orlando's airport) 24 hours before your flight to make arrangements for someone to help with your luggage and to provide for your own Transportation. inside the airport.

Driving

For many families, a road trip is the way to go. There is often less cost, you can pack more of what you need, and you have your car at the resort if you need anything.

- If you need to break the trip up, have a hotel booked. Sometimes towns you never expect to fill up have unexpected crowds because of college graduations, parents weekends, or NASCAR races.
- Pack Ziploc bags and wipes in the car (have them handy).
- Don't promise a certain lunch or dinner if you aren't certain there will be one. Chipotle and Chick-fil-A aren't everywhere, although McDonalds seems safe.
- Make a playlist or have a stack of CDs ready. Music can set the mood for the trip.
- Keep the noise-reducing headphones handy. Public restrooms can be loud.
- Check Pinterest for fun ideas (if you are at least a little crafty).
- Keep items for service animals handy, too.

Travel in Orlando

My family has always traveled I-75 south to the Florida Turnpike then followed the signs. In the days of technology, where everyone has a GPS on their phone or in their car, I won't bother you with instructions. However, I do want you to know the best route is a toll road. Be prepared with singles and quarters for three stops and a total of $5.75 in tolls (one way). You don't need exact change, but you do need cash. If you have an EZ Pass from up north, it won't translate yet, but they say it's coming soon. If you have a Sun Pass, Georgia's Peach Pass, or North Carolina's Quick Pass, you don't need to stop, Florida will just send you the bill.

If you're not renting a car, you have a few other options:

Magical Express. Magical Express is a benefit of staying on Disney property. Plush passenger buses with TVs that play Disney cartoons and promotional videos pick you up at the Orlando airport and take you directly to your Disney resort. There are times when a bus waits a while to fill up before leaving, and they do stop at as many as three resorts, but you don't have to worry about a thing, including your luggage. Your luggage will magically arrive in your hotel room after your arrival (sometimes a couple of hours later, so pack accordingly).

If you need a handicapped accessible bus, let them know when you book your reservation. This really is the best option if you need wheelchair accessible transportation.

At the Orlando International Airport, follow the signs to baggage claim, then skip it, and follow the signs to Magical Express. Cast members will scan your MagicBand and direct you from there. It's that easy, and free.

Car Service. Some families want to make a few stops, like for groceries, or don't want to wait the extra time for Magical Express. Many car services are available to pick you up at the airport, stop at the grocery store (sometimes for an additional fee, sometimes not), and take you directly to your resort. If you need a car seat or other special accommodation, there's usually an additional charge. Car services can be expensive; shop around and read reviews online..

Uber. In 2017 Uber and Lyft were added to the services offered at Orlando International Airport (MCO). Have your app downloaded and ready before you leave home to prevent hassles at the airport.

CHAPTER FOUR

Selecting Your Home Away from Home

In this chapter, I will explain the magical, great, and not-so-great aspects of the Disney resort hotels and review them based on accessibility and sensory needs.

Each hotel can earn up to four stars in these categories:

- *Accessible*. All resorts are accessible (some are just more friendly to navigate than others). The stars how well the hotel has implemented the accessibility features it is required to have, and the overall friendliness of the cast members to guests with special needs.
- *Quiet*. Some resorts are super quiet (think cabins and tree houses away from it all), others will be a little noise, and some will be loud. More stars equals more quiet.
- *Convenient*. Dining options, transportation options, and location.
- *Family-oriented*. Layout, formality, pools, etc.

Staying on Property. Convenience is the best word to describe the benefits of staying on property. Amazing customer service and never having to leave the Disney bubble are wonderful bonuses, too. Here are some other benefits:

- *Location*. You can leave the parks for naps and breaks without needing to get in a car or hassle with parking lots; plus, it's so close!
- *MagicBands*. A MagicBand is a silicone bracelet that is your room key, park tickets, FP+, and charge card all in one. My family loves it so much we miss it when we re-emerge into the real world. It really is great not having to dig into a bag or your pocket for what you need. If a member of your party doesn't want to wear a MagicBand, a parent can wear two bands, or the band can be hooked onto a bag or stroller. You can even turn your MagicBand into a lanyard.

- *Early FastPass+ (FP+).* If you are a resort guest, you may schedule all of your FP+ 60 days before your stay begins. If you aren't on property, you have only 30 days before each day of your vacation. You also only have to sit down once at the computer to set up your FP+s. Guests staying off property have to set up their FP+ each day 30 days out from visiting the park.
- *Advanced Dinner Reservations (ADRs).* For certain restaurants you do need to book your reservation 6 months out. If you are staying on property, you can make reservations for your whole vacation 180 days out. So again, you get a headstart over non-resort guests. Do not promise you will eat with princesses, Beast, or Doc McStuffins until you have a reservation.
- *Transportation.* My husband loves to arrive at Disney World and not have to think about driving, parking, or how to get someplace. There are buses, monorails, boats, and the Magical Express that will get you everywhere you need to be, even to and from the airport, and it's all free! *Note*: The resorts off property that provide shuttles are not fully accessible. They will not carry ECV's or foldable wheelchairs. They only have service available for electric standard wheelchairs.
- *Free Parking.* If you do need or want to drive, parking is free to all guests staying on property, anywhere in the resort.
- *Extra Magic Hours.* Each park has days they either open early or stay open late for guests staying on property. We're early risers, and we can get a lot accomplished during morning Extra Magic Hours. Many families like the late hours, especially if you want to enjoy a long break during the day. Check the Disney Parks website to see park hours for when you are traveling.

For guests with disabilities, Disney offers:

- Free valet parking to cars with handicapped tags or license plates
- Lifts or zero entry in all of the pools
- Rooms with visual alarms, doorbell indicators, and TTY by request
- Accessible rooms for wheelchairs

How to Book an Accessible Room. You can call the reservation number at (407) 939-5277 and ask for an accessible room, or if you would rather book online, click the box marked accessible rooms right next to the dates you would like to travel. The rooms that come up will have different accommodations including rooms for hearing impaired and rooms for service animals as well as wheelchair accessible bathrooms, read carefully before you book.

Service Animals, defined by Disney as "any dog or miniature horse trained to do work or perform tasks for the benefit of an individual with a disability," are of course welcome almost anywhere on Disney property with the guest they assist. There are no extra fees for a service dog or miniature horse that is licensed with a harness. It is more likely now that proper paperwork is shown because of the new pet policy.

Pet Dogs are now welcome in four of the Disney resorts: Art of Animation, Port Orleans Riverside, Cabins at Fort Wilderness, and the Yacht Club.

- There is a two-dog maximum per room.
- They will need to have proof of up-to-date vaccinations.
- There is a cleaning fee added per night.
- The pets must not be left unattended more than seven hours.
- Your room will be easily accessible to relief and walking areas.
- A Pluto tag door hanger will be provided to alert Housekeeping that they are there. You will need to schedule cleanings when your dog is out or you are there with them.
- You will receive a package containing a bowl, ID tag, disposable bags, a mat, puppy pads, and a map for walking.
- You will be responsible for cleaning up after your dog(s).
- No pets are allowed in dining locations, pool areas, on lobby furniture, or other marked public areas.
- Pets are not allowed in the parks or Disney Springs.
- If there are noise complaints, you will be asked to attend to your pet within 30 minutes.
- Pet dogs are allowed in Magical Express and the Minnie Vans. They must remain in a carrier at all times.

If you are planning a day that will not allow you to get back to your room in seven hours, there is a great kennel with daycare services on property. www.bestfriendpetcare.com

This policy is currently running on a trial basis. All reservations through October 15, 2018, will be accepted.

Choosing a Disney Property Resort. There are 21 properties and a campground at WDW. The benefits listed above are available at all of them, with a wide range of convenience, amenities, and cost.

Disney has four categories for their resorts.

- *Deluxe Villas.* These are rooms that include kitchenettes, living areas, and more space than standard rooms. If you choose a studio, it is basically a deluxe room without the extra living space. The accommodations are grand, and most of them have different transportation available in addition to the buses. Many times these villas are used by guests who belong to the Disney Vacation Club (a type of time share).

- *Deluxe Resorts.* Deluxe resorts have plush accommodations, more square footage in the rooms, upgraded toiletries, and even nicer toilet paper. They offer inside hallways and a more traditional "hotel feel." Most have the restaurants, a reservation desk, and rooms connected with elegantly decorated hallways. Most also have additional types of transportation, such as the monorail or boats.
- *Moderate Resorts.* Moderate resorts have comfortable rooms, great food courts for eating options, and nice amenities, and most of them have boat transportation to one location and cool spaces outside for exploring. Most of the moderate resorts are very spread out with multiple buildings of rooms, then a main building where the food court, guest services, and gift shops are located. There is one large pool with a slide, activities, and music. Some of them also have quiet pools that are closer to your rooms with less traffic and commotion.
- *Value Resorts.* These resorts are more basic. The rooms are smaller, there are fewer amenities, and although there is still a lot of magic, there aren't as many comfortable touches, like a covered bus stop with benches.
- *Disney Campgrounds.* These are campsites for tents or RVs. They have all the basic amenities like electric hook up and free Wi-Fi.

Deluxe Resorts

- *Best Value.* Fort Wilderness Lodge.
- *Best Location.* A three-way tie between the "monorail resorts: Grand Floridian, Contemporary, Polynesian.
- *Amy's Pick.* Fort Wilderness Lodge. Nice location, easy accessibility, great dining option, quiet, boat to Magic Kingdom and nice bus stop, including a walkway with overhead cover.

Disney's Grand Floridian Resort and Spa

Accessible ★★★★ Quiet ★★★ Convenient ★★★★ Overall ★★★

The Grand Floridian is the flagship property of Walt Disney World. The amenities and the price points reflect that. It's a beautiful resort that brings you back to the Victorian age, with beautiful gardens, lattice work, turrets, white walls, light décor, and a stunning red roof that pulls it all together. The lobby has beautiful crystal chandeliers and a dramatic staircase.

Rooms. These are some of the largest rooms at WDW, with 2 queen beds, a daybed, and a small table with 2 chairs. Decorated in a traditional Victorian theme. The bathrooms are split (2 sinks and a dressing area are separated from the shower and toilet) with nice counter space and shelving for storage. The towels and toiletries are high quality. There are balconies or patios with 2 chairs and a small table. Rooms accommodate 5 adults and 1 child under 3.

Amenities include:

- Free Wi-Fi
- Hair dryer
- Coffee maker
- Phone with voice mail
- Small in-room safe
- Mini refrigerator
- Ironing board/iron
- Pack 'n' play
- USB ports and outlets on nightstand
- H20 brand shampoo, conditioner, shower gel, lotion, facial soap, and bar soap for the sink

The accessible rooms have a variety of options. Some include hearing accessibility, some have a roll-in shower, others have tubs with bars. Not all of the rooms have ADA-recommended heights for dressers, tables, and countertops. Most rooms have 2 queen beds, but all of the rooms with the roll-in shower option have 1 king bed.

You are able to choose a room online with the accommodations that work best for your family. When you click on "room rates," options for different rooms come up. Click the little box that says "accessible rooms." If you are more comfortable speaking with a Disney cast member, call reservations at (407) 939-5277 and explain which accommodations you need.

Transportation. The monorail or a boat will take you directly to the Magic Kingdom, and the monorail will also take you to the TTC (Transportation & Ticket Center) where you can transfer for a monorail to Epcot. Buses take you to Animal Kingdom, Hollywood Studios, the water parks, and Disney Springs.

Dining. There are several dining choices ranging from 24-hour counter service to signature five-diamond dining with a dress code.

- *Victoria and Albert's.* This is a very fancy and very expensive restaurant. If your budget and your family are able to experience a true dining event, enjoy! There is a dress code. Gentlemen must wear a tie and jacket and ladies must wear a nice dress or pant outfit. No tennis shoes, flip-flops, shorts, or jeans are permitted. This dress code is strictly enforced.

- *Citrico's.* $$$, fine dining, dinner only.
- *Narcoossee's.* $$$, fine dining, dinner only.
- *Grand Floridian Café.* $$, casual dining, table service.
- *1900 Park Fare.* $$. $$$, character dining.
- *Garden View Tea Room.* $$$, character dining/special events.
- *Gasparilla Island Grille.* $, counter service, open 24 hours.
- *Mizner's Lounge.* Bar with live music.
- *Courtyard Pool Bar.* $, drinks, limited menu.
- *Beach Pool Bar.* $, drinks, limited menu.

Recreation. Recreation options include:

- *Pools.* There are two pools. Both are zero entry, making it easy for accessibility and great for little ones to play. The Courtyard Pool is the quieter option. It has a water slide and a splash area (some squirters in the zero entry), but not the activities, music, and games. The pool area also includes a spa (hot tub). The Beach Pool is closer to the Villas and it attracts guests that like more activity. There are games, music, and other activities, plus an Alice in Wonderland-themed water play area with slides and water fun. Cabanas are available to rent. Water wings are welcome and there are life jackets available for you to borrow. There is also a gift shop where sunscreen, goggles, and pool toys are available in case you forgot anything.
- *Arcade.* Classic and modern arcade games and air hockey. Florida law prohibits games that dispense tickets for prizes.
- *Movies under the stars.* Watch Disney movies outside under the stars. There's a schedule for movies near the pool and at the concierge desk.
- *Campfire.* Come listen to campfire stories and roast marshmallows..
- *Jogging trail.* Marked, paved jogging trail.
- *Motorized boat rentals.* The marina has jet skis and small boats you can rent to pilot on the Seven Seas Lagoon, for a fee, with reservations accepted.
- *Bass fishing.* Guided fishing excursion on the Seven Seas Lagoon, for a fee, with reservations accepted.
- *Note*: there is no playground at the Grand Floridian.

Amy's Analysis. The Grand Floridian certainly lives up to its name; it is grand. Every Disney resort welcomes families and children; however, the hushed tones and formal setting of this resort can make it uncomfortable for families dealing with frequent meltdowns, which might feel more noticeable here than at other resorts. There is also not as big a "Disney magic" feel. The décor is more Victorian and formal, and some families might appreciate a little more separation to calm down a bit. This is a quiet and not over-stimulating resort, with convenient elevators.

Disney's Contemporary Resort

Accessible ★★★★ Quiet ★★ Convenient ★★★★ Overall ★★★

The Contemporary Resort is the hotel you see in the commercials where the monorail comes into the resort. The kids *love* it. There is a very modern feel; however, I don't find it futuristic or uncomfortable.

Rooms. Large rooms, most have 2 queen beds, a daybed, and a small table with 2 chairs. Decorated in clean, modern decor. The bathrooms are split (2 sinks and a dressing area are separated from the shower and toilet) with nice counter space and shelving for storage. The towels and toiletries are high quality. There are balconies or patios with 2 chairs and a small table. Rooms accommodate 5 adults and 1 child under 3.

Amenities include:

- Free Wi-Fi
- Hair dryer
- Coffee maker
- Phone with voice mail
- Small in-room safe
- Mini refrigerator
- Ironing board/iron
- Pack 'n' play
- USB ports and outlets on nightstand
- H20 brand shampoo, conditioner, shower gel, lotion and facial soap, and bar soap for the sink.

The accessible rooms have a variety of options. Some include hearing accessibility, some have a roll-in shower, others have tubs with bars. Not all of the rooms have ADA-recommended heights for dressers, tables, and countertops. Most rooms have 2 queen beds, but all of the rooms with the roll-in shower option have 1 king bed.

You are able to choose a room online with the accommodations that work best for your family. When you click on "room rates," options for different rooms come up. Click the little box that says "accessible rooms." If you are more comfortable speaking with a Disney cast member, call reservations at (407) 939-5277 and explain which accommodations you need.

Transportation. The monorail or a boat ride will take you directly to the Magic Kingdom, and the monorail will also take you to the TTC where you can transfer for a monorail to Epcot. Buses take you to Animal Kingdom, Hollywood Studios, the water parks, and Disney Springs.

Dining. There are several dining choices ranging from 24-hour counter service to signature dining.

- *California Grill.* $$$, fine dining, dinner only.
- *The Wave...of American Flavors.* $$, casual dining, table service.
- *Contempo Grounds.* $, coffee shop.
- *Chef Mickey's.* $$-$$$, character dining.
- *Contempo Café.* $, counter service., open 24 hours.
- *Outer Rim Lounge Bar.* $, poolside food.
- *The Sand Bar.* $, poolside food.
- *Cove Bar.* $, poolside, drinks, limited menu.
- *Wave Lounge.* $, drinks, limited menu.

Recreation. Recreation options include:

- *Pools.* There are two pool options. The feature pool has a water slide, activities, and music. There is a hot tub, water play area with fountains, and a kiddie pool. There are also cabanas to rent. The Bay Pool is the quiet option where loud noises and splashing are "gently discouraged."
- *Arcade.* Classic and modern arcade games and air hockey. A Florida law prohibits games that dispense tickets for prizes.
- *Movies under the stars.* Watch Disney movies outside under the stars. There's a schedule for movies near the pool and at the concierge desk.
- *Campfire.* Come listen to campfire stories and roast marshmallows.
- *Jogging trail. Marked, paved jogging trail.*
- *Bass fishing.* Guided fishing excursion on the Seven Seas Lagoon, for a fee, with reservations accepted.
- *Other Activities.* Tennis, volleyball. T
- *Note:* there is no playground at the Contemporary.

Amy's Analysis. The Contemporary Resort is a lot of fun. Sometimes fun can be a little noisy. The height of the main tower allows sound to travel up, and the activity from conventions, Chef Mickey's, and the monorail can be deafening. I suggest a room in the garden wing, which is both quieter and less expensive than the tower. This resort is accessible friendly.

Disney's Polynesian Resort

Accessible ★★★★ Quiet ★★★ Convenient ★★★★ Overall ★★★

Welcome to paradise, and a resort that makes you feel as if you really got away to a lazy tropical island. The Polynesian is a favorite among families that love a Tiki theme. Lilo, Stitch, and Moana are the featured characters. There is a volcano at the pool and a luau dinner to add to the theme.

Rooms. Large rooms, most have 2 queen beds, a daybed, and a small table with 2 chairs. Decorated in an island theme. The bathrooms are split (2 sinks and a dressing area are separated from the shower and toilet) with nice counter space and shelving for storage. The towels and toiletries are high quality. There are balconies or patios with 2 chairs and a small table. Rooms with a daybed can accommodate 5 adults and 1 child under 3.

Amenities include:

- Free Wi-Fi
- Hair dryer
- Coffee maker
- Phone with voice mail
- Small in-room safe
- Mini refrigerator
- Ironing board/iron
- Pack 'n' play
- USB ports and outlets on nightstand
- H20 brand shampoo, conditioner, shower gel, lotion and facial soap, and bar soap for the sink.

The accessible rooms have a variety of options. Some include hearing accessibility, some have a roll-in shower, others have tubs with bars. Not all of the rooms have ADA-recommended heights for dressers, tables, and countertops. Most rooms have 2 queen beds, but all of the rooms with the roll-in shower option have 1 king bed.

You are able to choose a room online with the accommodations that work best for your family. When you click on "room rates," options for different rooms come up. Click the little box that says "accessible rooms." If you are more comfortable speaking with a Disney cast member, call reservations at (407) 939-5277 and explain which accommodations you need.

Transportation. The monorail or a boat ride will take you directly to the Magic Kingdom, and the monorail will also take you to the TTC where you can transfer for a monorail to Epcot. Buses take you to Animal Kingdom, Hollywood Studios, the water parks, and Disney Springs.

Dining. There are several dining choices ranging from 24-hour counter service to signature dining.

- *The Spirit of America.* $$$$, dinner show (luau).
- *Ohana's.* $$-$$$, character dining.
- *Captain Cooks.* $, counter service.
- *Tambu Lounge Bar.* $, drinks.
- *Oasis Bar and Grill.* $, poolside food.
- *Barefoot Pool.* $, poolside, drinks.
- *Kohana Island.* $, sushi.
- *Pineapple Lanai.* $, Dole Whip.
- *Trader Sam's Tiki Bar.* $$, drinks, food.

Recreation. Recreation options include:

- *Pools.* There are two pool options. The Lava Pool is zero entry and has a water slide, activities, music, and a volcano. The Oasis Pool is the quiet option where loud noises and splashing are "gently discouraged."
- *Arcade.* Classic and modern arcade games and air hockey. A Florida law prohibits games that dispense tickets for prizes.
- *Movies under the stars.* Watch Disney movies outside under the stars. There's a schedule for movies near the pool and at the concierge desk.
- *Campfire.* Come listen to campfire stories and roast marshmallows.
- *Jogging trail.* Marked, paved jogging trail.
- *Bass fishing.* Guided fishing excursion on the Seven Seas Lagoon, for a fee, with reservations accepted.
- *Other activities.* Volleyball, motorized boat rentals to pilot yourself on the Seven Seas Lagoon.
- *Note*: there is no playground at the Polynesian Resort.

Amy's Analysis. The Polynesian is a fun resort, especially if you enjoy the Polynesian theme. The lobby can be a little busy. It's smaller than the lobby and monorail areas at the Contemporary and Grand Floridian. The tropical feel of the resort creates more of an "I've escaped" feeling. The resort is accessible, if not quite as easy as the Contemporary to navigate. There is more hustle and bustle, but still a quiet resort.

Disney's Wilderness Lodge

Accessible ★★★★ Quiet ★★★ Convenient ★★★★ Overall ★★★★

As you enter the Fort Wilderness Lodge, you feel as if you have arrived out west to Yellowstone National Park, complete with a geyser.

Rooms. Large rooms, most have 2 queen beds, a daybed, and a small table with 2 chairs. There are also rooms with 1 queen and a bunk bed. Decorated in a Southwest theme in blues and greens. The bathrooms are split (2 sinks and a dressing area are separated from the shower and toilet) with nice counter space and shelving for storage. The towels and toiletries are high quality. There are balconies or patios with 2 chairs and a small table. Rooms with a daybed can accommodate 5 adults and 1 child under 3.

Amenities include:

- Free Wi-Fi
- Hair dryer
- Coffee maker
- Phone with voice mail
- Small in-room safe
- Mini refrigerator
- Ironing board/iron
- Pack 'n' play
- USB ports and outlets on nightstand
- H20 brand shampoo, conditioner, shower gel, lotion and facial soap, and bar soap for the sink.

The accessible rooms have a variety of options. Some include hearing accessibility, some have a roll-in shower, others have tubs with bars. Not all of the rooms have ADA-recommended heights for dressers, tables, and countertops. Most rooms have 2 queen beds, but all of the rooms with the roll-in shower option have 1 king bed.

You are able to choose a room online with the accommodations that work best for your family. When you click on "room rates," options for different rooms come up. Click the little box that says "accessible rooms." If you are more comfortable speaking with a Disney cast member, call reservations at (407) 939-5277 and explain which accommodations you need.

Transportation. A boat is available to and from the Magic Kingdom and the Grand Floridian. There are buses to take you to all parks and Disney Springs.

Dining. There are several dining choices ranging from 24-hour counter service to signature dining.

- *Artist Point.* $$$, fine dining.
- *Whispering Canyon.* $-$$, table service.
- *Roaring Fork.* $, counter service.
- *Territory Lounge Bar.* $.
- *Oasis Bar and Grill.* $, poolside food.
- *Trout Pass.* $, poolside, drinks.

Recreation. Recreation options include:

- *Pools.* There are two pool options. The Silver Creek pool is settled into boulders and pine trees overlooking the Seven Seas Lagoon and a geyser. There's a water slide, activities, and music. The new Boulder Ridge Pool is zero entry, allowing for easier entrance, and it will have a beautiful new sundeck and décor that looks like it's settled into a rock quarry.
- *Arcade.* Classic and modern arcade games and air hockey. A Florida law prohibits games that dispense tickets for prizes.
- *Movies under the stars.* Watch Disney movies outside under the stars. There's a schedule for movies near the pool and at the concierge desk.
- *Campfire.* Come listen to campfire stories and roast marshmallows.
- *Jogging trail.* Marked, paved jogging trail.
- *Bass fishing.* Guided fishing excursion on the Seven Seas Lagoon, for a fee, with reservations accepted.
- *Other activities.* Playground, bike rentals, motorized boat rentals to pilot yourself on the Seven Seas Lagoon.

Amy's Analysis. Disney's Wilderness Lodge is my family's favorite. It is a nice size, has good dining options, and the location and theming are great. The walkway to the bus stop has a slight ramp that is covered providing shade and protection from the rain. Until sometime in the summer of 2017, you need to go to the nearby Fort Wilderness campsites to enjoy movies under the stars and campfires (with Chip and Dale). There was construction while we were there in summer 2016, and it didn't bother us at all. It might have even been why the crowds were low. Accessibility is friendly and the resort is quiet.

Disney's Animal Kingdom Lodge

Accessible ★★★★ Quiet ★★★ Convenient ★★★ Overall ★★★

There is nothing cooler than looking out the window and seeing live giraffes and zebras. At the Animal Kingdom Lodge, you can see them everywhere, even outside the balcony in your room. Add to that a beautiful setting and décor plus unique dining options, and Animal Kingdom Lodge is very cool. This resort is separated into two areas: Jambo House which has more traditional rooms and suites, and Kidani Village, where the DVC rooms are more like apartments. An internal shuttle operates between the two.

Rooms. Large rooms, most have 2 queen beds, a daybed, and a small table with 2 chairs. Decorated in earth colors and African themes. There are rooms with 1 queen and a bunk bed. The bathrooms are split (2 sinks and a dressing area are separated from the shower and toilet) with nice counter space and shelving for storage. The towels and toiletries are high quality. There are balconies or patios with 2 chairs and a small table. Rooms with the day bed can accommodate 5 adults and 1 child under 3.

Amenities include:

- Free Wi-Fi
- Hair dryer
- Coffee maker
- Phone with voice mail
- Small in-room safe
- Mini refrigerator
- Ironing board/iron
- Pack 'n' play
- USB ports and outlets on nightstand
- H20 brand shampoo, conditioner, shower gel, lotion and facial soap, and bar soap for the sink

The accessible rooms have a variety of options. Some include hearing accessibility, some have a roll-in shower, others have tubs with bars. Not all of the accessible rooms have ADA-recommended heights for dressers, tables, and countertops. Most rooms have 2 queen beds, but all of the rooms with the roll-in shower option have 1 king bed.

You are able to choose a room online with the accommodations that work best for your family. When you click on "room rates," options for different rooms come up. Click the little box that says "accessible rooms." If you are more comfortable speaking with a Disney cast member, call reservations at (407) 939-5277 and explain which accommodations you need.

Unless you choose a room with a view of the Arusha Savannah (not inexpensive), do not promise your family there will be zebras and giraffes outside their window. The other savannah rooms are also beautiful, and have exotic animals but not always zebras or giraffes. There are many areas both inside and outside where you can view the animals; if your budget won't stretch for the savannah views I still recommend this resort if you have animal lovers in your group.

Transportation. Animal Kingdom Lodge only has buses available for transportation to all of the parks and Disney Springs.

Dining. There are several dining choices ranging from 24-hour counter service to signature dining.

- *Jiko.* $$$, fine dining.
- *Boma: Flavors of Africa.* $$-$$$, table service (buffet).
- *Sanaa.* $$ table service.
- *The Mara.* $, counter service.
- *Cape Town Wine and Lounge.* $, drinks.
- *Victoria Falls Lounge.* $, drinks.
- *Maji.* $, poolside food, and bar.
- *Uzima Springs Poolside Bar.* $, drinks.

Recreation. Recreation options include:

- *Pools.* There are two large zero-entry pools with nearby spas. Uzima is a zero-entry pool with a water slide. Samawati, the pool with more activities and games, is a large water play area near the Villas. (It's quite a walk if you are in the lodge.)
- *Arcade.* Classic and modern arcade games and air hockey. A Florida law prohibits games that dispense tickets for prizes.
- *Movies under the stars.* Watch Disney movies outside under the stars. There's a schedule for movies near the pool and at the concierge desk.
- *Campfire.* Come listen to campfire stories and roast marshmallows.
- *Jogging trail.* Marked, paved jogging trail.
- *Other activities.* Playground, various activities that involve spotting and watching animals.

Amy's Analysis. The Animal Kingdom Lodge is a magnificent resort. The reasons it isn't my favorite are convenience and value. It is located near Animal Kingdom and Blizzard Beach, but that's about it. The buses take awhile to reach the other parks. Also, the counter-service area is not very convenient to get to. It's all the way to the lowest level, then around a bend and outside. My other thought about Animal Kingdom is the pool at Jambo House. There is a fence around it that is great for keeping kids from running from the dining area into the pool, however, it cuts up the pool area in such a way that you can not walk around the whole perimeter of the pool without having to go out the fence and walk around. If you have one child in the zero entry and another at the slide, it gets complicated. The pool area at Kidani is better set up, so I would consider the internal shuttle for a pool day. But, giraffes and zebras! If that will excite your family, do consider Animal Kingdom Lodge.

Disney's BoardWalk Inn

Accessible ★★ Quiet ★★★ Convenient ★★ Overall ★★

The waterfront setting with manicured gardens, the beautiful pastel-colored buildings with elegant balconies, and the liveliness and activity of the Boardwalk bring you back in time to turn-of-the-last-century Atlantic City. The BoardWalk has a fabulous location, within walking distance to Epcot and just a little farther walk to Hollywood Studios. Plus, there is a boat ride that will take you to either park. The interior and rooms are just as beautiful and appealing as the exterior. However, there are a few things that make this resort less convenient. The dining is all located outside on the Boardwalk. The counter service is limited to pizza and a bakery, and to get outside there are steps in every direction. A ramp and elevator are available, but out of the way. Then there is the questionable decision of putting a large clown face as a central part of the pool décor. I know quite a few people that fear or at least dislike clowns. My friend and I enjoyed our stay, but we have no mobility challenges and we were traveling without children.

Rooms. Large rooms, most have 2 queen beds, a daybed, and a small table with 2 chairs. Beautifully decorated rooms in a turn-of-the-last-century feel. The bathrooms are split (2 sinks and a dressing area are separated from the shower and toilet) with nice counter space and shelving for storage. The towels and toiletries are high quality. There are balconies or patios with 2 chairs and a small table. Rooms with the day bed can accommodate 5 adults and 1 child under 3.

Amenities include:

- Free Wi-Fi
- Hair dryer
- Coffee maker
- Phone with voice mail
- Small in-room safe
- Mini refrigerator
- Ironing board/iron
- Pack 'n' play
- USB ports and outlets on nightstand
- H20 brand shampoo, conditioner, shower gel, lotion and facial soap, and bar soap for the sink.

The accessible rooms have a variety of options. Some include hearing accessibility, some have a roll-in shower, others have tubs with bars. Not all of the rooms have ADA-recommended heights for dressers, tables, and countertops. Most rooms have 2 queen beds, but all of the rooms with the roll-in shower option have 1 king bed.

You are able to choose a room online with the accommodations that work best for your family. When you click on "room rates," options for different rooms come up. Click the little box that says "accessible rooms." If you are more comfortable speaking with a Disney cast member, call reservations at (407) 939-5277 and explain which accommodations you need.

Transportation. There are good options for transportation at the BoardWalk. A boat is available for Epcot and Hollywood Studios, buses take you anywhere else, but the nicest option is a quick stroll to Epcot and a nice walk to Hollywood Studios.

Dining. I find the dining options to be limited. All of the options except room service require going to the Boardwalk or the pool bar.

- *Flying Fish.* $$$, fine dining, dress code, dinner only.
- *Big River Grill and Brew Works.* $$-$$$, table service.
- *ESPN Club.* $$, table service.
- *Trattoria al Forno.* $-$$, table service, breakfast, lunch, and dinner.
- *Boardwalk Bakery.* $, counter service.
- *Pizza Window.* $, counter service, lunch and dinner.

Recreation. Recreation options include:

- *Pools.* The signature pool area has a water slide that reminds you of the old roller coasters: there are spraying elephants and a carnival theme, and a bar that looks like a carousel. I do need to say that the that the carnival includes a *large* clown face. There are also two quiet pools. They are both surrounded by beautiful gardens, have lifts for wheelchairs, and "gently discourage" splashing and noise.
- *Arcade.* Classic and modern arcade games and air hockey. A Florida law prohibits games that dispense tickets for prizes.
- *Movies under the stars.* Watch Disney movies outside under the stars. There's a schedule for movies near the pool and at the concierge desk.
- *Campfire.* Come listen to campfire stories and roast marshmallows.
- *Jogging trail.* Marked, paved jogging trail.
- *Other activities.* Tennis, bike rentals, playground, bass fishing excursions.
- *Note:* Fantasia Gardens (mini golf) is nearby.

Amy's Analysis. The BoardWalk Inn is hard to pin down. It's a beautiful, plush resort with a fabulous location, but for families or guests with mobility, sensory, or dining issues, there are better options.

Disney's Beach Club Resort

Accessible ★★★ Quiet ★★★ Convenient ★★★ Overall ★★★

The Beach Club and her sister resort, the Yacht Club, are joined in the middle and are very similar, especially since they share the same restaurants and main pool area. The Beach Club has brighter colors and a less formal feel, plus a fabulous location within walking distance of Epcot and Hollywood Studios.

Rooms. Large rooms, most have 2 queen beds, a daybed, and a small table with 2 chairs. Beautifully decorated rooms in light beachy colors and a nautical theme. The bathrooms are split (2 sinks and a dressing area are separated from the shower and toilet) with nice counter space and shelving for storage. The towels and toiletries are high quality. There are balconies or patios with 2 chairs and a small table. The balconies at the Yacht Club are larger than the balconies at the Beach Club. Rooms with day beds can accommodate 5 adults and 1 child under 3.

Amenities include:

- Free Wi-Fi
- Hair dryer
- Coffee maker
- Phone with voice mail
- Small in-room safe
- Mini refrigerator
- Ironing board/iron
- Pack 'n' play
- USB ports and outlets on nightstand
- H20 brand shampoo, conditioner, shower gel, lotion and facial soap, and bar soap for the sink

The accessible rooms have a variety of options. Some include hearing accessibility, some have a roll-in shower, others have tubs with bars. Not all of the rooms have ADA-recommended heights for dressers, tables, and countertops. Most rooms have 2 queen beds, but all of the rooms with the roll-in shower option have 1 king bed.

You are able to choose a room online with the accommodations that work best for your family. When you click on "room rates," options for different rooms come up. Click the little box that says "accessible rooms." If you are more comfortable speaking with a Disney cast member, call reservations at (407) 939-5277 and explain which accommodations you need.

Transportation. A boat is available for Epcot and Hollywood Studios, buses are available for all parks and Disney Springs, but the nicest option is a short walk to Hollywood Studios or Epcot.

Dining. I find the dining options to be limited. There isn't a designated counter-service option for all three meals. The Beach Club Marketplace is hidden in a gift shop (that can be very distracting and lead to melt downs) and the seating is outside. Then there is a limited menu in the soda shop, but again, melt downs, and there are no breakfast options.

- *Yachtsmen Steakhouse.* $$$, fine dining, dress code, dinner only.
- *Cape May Café.* $$-$$$, character meal, table service, breakfast and lunch.
- *Captains Grille.* $$, table service.
- *Hurricane Hannah's.* $, pool bar.
- *Beaches and Cream Soda Shop.* $, counter service, lunch and dinner.
- *Beaches Marketplace.* $, counter service, breakfast, lunch, and dinner.

Recreation. Recreation options include:

- *Pools.* Storm-a-Long Bay is the name of the very popular pool complex shared by the Beach and Yacht Club resorts. There is a lazy river and a whirlpool, a cool slide that come off a ship wreck, a sandbar area that has a sandy bottom, "dunes" that provide plenty of space and sand to make sand castles, and shallow water to splash around in. There are noodles and tubes available for rent to enjoy in the lazy river. If you are driving to WDW and have room for a couple of noodles, I would throw them in the car. *Note:* The entire pool has a sand bottom. Most guests think this is amazing because it is more comfortable for their feet. I see it as a sensory and mobility challenge. Some guests will have a harder time with sand. Also, this pool is so popular that Disney is strict about only allowing access only to Beach and Yacht Club guests. There are three quiet pools. They are all surrounded by beautiful gardens, have lifts for wheelchairs, and "gently discourage" splashing and noise.
- *Arcade.* Classic and modern arcade games and air hockey. A Florida law prohibits games that dispense tickets for prizes.
- *Movies under the stars.* Watch Disney movies outside under the stars. There's a schedule for movies near the pool and at the concierge desk.
- *Campfire.* Come listen to campfire stories and roast marshmallows.

- *Jogging trail.* Marked, paved jogging trail.
- *Other activities.* Tennis, volleyball, boat rentals, bike rentals, bass fishing excursions.
- *Note:* Fantasia Gardens (mini golf) is nearby.
- *Note:* there is no playground at the Beach or Yacht Club resorts.

Amy's Analysis. The Beach Club has some very fun features and a great location. However, there are fewer dining options and the pool can either be the best pool at a WDW resort, or challenging.

Disney's Yacht Club Resort

Accessible ★★★★ Quiet ★★★ Convenient ★★★★ Overall ★★

The Yacht Club can feel just a little more formal than her sister resort, the Beach Club. Yet they are very similar and share boat launches, the main pool, and dining. The Yacht Club's balconies are better. This is a pet friendly resort accepting up to 2 pet dogs per room for an additional $75/night fee.

Rooms. Large rooms, most have 2 queen beds, a daybed, and a small table with 2 chairs. Nicely decorated rooms in blues and grays and a nautical theme. The bathrooms are split (2 sinks and a dressing area are separated from the shower and toilet) with nice counter space and shelving for storage. The towels and toiletries are high quality. There are balconies or patios with 2 chairs and a small table. The balconies at Yacht Club are larger than those at the Beach Club. Rooms with day beds can accommodate 5 adults and 1 child under 3.

Amenities include:

- Free Wi-Fi
- Hair dryer
- Coffee maker
- Phone with voice mail
- Small in-room safe
- Mini refrigerator
- Ironing board/iron
- Pack 'n' play
- USB ports and outlets on nightstand
- H20 brand shampoo, conditioner, shower gel, lotion and facial soap, and bar soap for the sink

The accessible rooms have a variety of options. Some include hearing accessibility, some have a roll-in shower, others have tubs with bars. Not all of the rooms have ADA-recommended heights for dressers, tables, and countertops. Most rooms have 2 queen beds, but all of the rooms with the roll-in shower option have 1 king bed.

You are able to choose a room online with the accommodations that work best for your family. When you click on "room rates," options for different rooms come up. Click the little box that says "accessible rooms." If you are more comfortable speaking with a Disney cast member, call reservations at (407) 939-5277 and explain which accommodations you need.

Transportation. There are good options for transportation. A boat is available for Epcot and Hollywood Studios, buses are available for all parks and Disney Springs, but the nicest option is a short walk to Hollywood Studios or Epcot.

Dining. I find the dining options to be limited. There isn't a designated counter-service option for all three meals. The Beach Club Marketplace is hidden in a gift shop (that can be very distracting and lead to melt downs) and the seating is outside with overhead cover. There is a limited menu in the soda shop, but again, melt downs, and no breakfast options.

- *Yachtsman Steakhouse.* $$$, Fine dining, dress code, dinner only.
- *Cape May Café.* $$. $$$, character meal, table service, breakfast and lunch.
- *Captain's Grille.* $$ table service.
- *Hurricane Hannah's.* $, pool bar.
- *Beaches and Cream Soda Shop.* $, counter service, lunch and dinner.
- Beaches Marketplace. $, counter service, breakfast, lunch and dinner.

Recreation. Recreation options include:

- Storm-a-Long Bay is the name of the very popular pool complex shared by the Beach and Yacht Club resorts. There is a lazy river and a whirlpool, a cool slide that come off a ship wreck, a sandbar area that has a sandy bottom, "dunes" that provide plenty of space and sand to make sand castles, and shallow water to splash around in. There are noodles and tubes available for rent to enjoy in the lazy river. If you are driving to WDW and have room for a couple of noodles, I would throw them in the car. *Note:* The entire pool has a sand bottom. Most guests think this is amazing because it is more comfortable for their feet. I see it as a sensory and mobility challenge. Some guests will have a harder time with sand. Also, this pool is so popular that Disney is strict about only allowing access only to Beach and Yacht Club guests. There are three quiet pools. They are all surrounded by beautiful gardens, have lifts for wheelchairs, and "gently discourage" splashing and noise. There are three quiet pools. They are all surrounded by beautiful gardens, have lifts for wheelchairs and "gently discourage" splashing and noise.

- *Arcade.* Classic and modern arcade games and air hockey. A Florida law prohibits games that dispense tickets for prizes.
- *Movies under the stars.* Watch Disney movies outside under the stars. There's a schedule for movies near the pool and at the concierge desk.
- *Campfire.* Come listen to campfire stories and roast marshmallows.
- *Jogging trail.* Marked, paved jogging trail.
- *Other activities.* Tennis, volleyball, boat rentals, bass fishing excursions.
- *Note:* Fantasia Gardens (mini golf) is nearby.
- *Note:* There is no playground at the Beach or Yacht Club resorts.

Amy's Analysis. The Yacht Club has some very fun features and a great location. However, there are fewer dining options, and the pet friendly status and pool can either be great options for your family, or it will be challenging.

Deluxe Villas

Most of the Deluxe resorts have a section of rooms that are considered Villas which have kitchenettes and living spaces and a variety of bedroom options. Most of the Villas include laundry facilities and more living space.

Bay Lake Resort at the Contemporary

Accessible ★★★★ Quiet ★★★ Convenient ★★★★ Overall ★★★★

Bay Lake is a stand-alone building with its own zero-entry pool that only Bay Tower guests may use. It is connected by a hallway to the Contemporary and shares its amenities and recreation. See the review of the Contemporary, above. Also, all rooms have fully stocked kitchenettes, and most (but not the studios) have a washer and dryer in the room.

Saratoga Springs Resort

Accessible ★★★★ Quiet ★★★★ Convenient ★★ Overall ★★★

Golfers, here is where you want to be. This is the only resort on a golf course (the other golf course is available for play, but the adjoining resort, Shades of Green, is reserved for military only). There are also tree houses here (well, suites on stilts situated in the trees). Inspired by the first American resorts in northern New York's horse country, Saratoga Springs is more reserved and quietly out of all the hustle and bustle many of the other resorts experience.

Rooms. All of the rooms are suites with a kitchen, living area, and bedrooms. Some of the rooms are in the main resort area (several buildings in a colony with a central building that house the lobby, restaurants, and gift shop). The other suites are called tree houses, upgraded cabins on stilts. The kids I know think they are very cool. Saratoga Springs is spread out. If you would like to be near the poo or lobby, ask for a room nearby.

Amenities include:

- Free Wi-Fi
- Hair dryer
- Coffee maker
- Phone with voice mail
- Small in-room safe
- Full-size refrigerator
- Microwave
- Toaster
- Cooking and eating utensils, pans, plates, etc.
- Washer and dryer (except in studio rooms)
- Ironing board/iron
- Pack 'n' play ask at desk
- USB ports and outlets on nightstand
- H20 brand shampoo, conditioner, shower gel, lotion and facial soap, and bar soap for the sink.

The accessible rooms have a variety of options. Some include hearing accessibility, some have a roll-in shower, others have tubs with bars. Not all of the rooms have ADA-recommended heights for dressers, tables, and countertops. Most rooms have 2 queen beds, but all of the rooms with the roll-in shower option have 1 king bed.

You are able to choose a room online with the accommodations that work best for your family. When you click on "room rates," options for different rooms come up. Click the little box that says "accessible rooms." If you are more comfortable speaking with a Disney cast member, call reservations at (407) 939-5277 and explain which accommodations you need.

Transportation. There are buses for all parks, and a boat and walking path to Disney Springs. The tree houses are more remote. There are 2 dedicated bus stops, but it can take a lot of time. A car (remember parking at all resorts and parks is free for guests) might be welcome at the tree houses.

Dining. Although it appears the dining is limited, every room has a kitchen, and you are a quick boat ride or walk to Disney Springs.

- *Turf Club Bar and Grille.* $$, table service.
- *Backstretch.* $, pool bar, lunch and dinner.
- *Paddock Grille.* $, counter service, breakfast, lunch, and dinner.
- *Artists Palette.* $, counter service, breakfast, lunch, and dinner.

Recreation. Recreation options include:

- *Pools.* There are 2 zero-entry pools with slides and snack bars (with bars). Many describe the pool scene as second only to the Beach and Yacht Club resorts.
- *Arcade.* Classic and modern arcade games and air hockey. A Florida law prohibits games that dispense tickets for prizes.
- *Movies under the stars.* Watch Disney movies outside under the stars. There's a schedule for movies near the pool and at the concierge desk.
- *Campfire.* Come listen to campfire stories and roast marshmallows.
- *Jogging trail.* Marked, paved jogging trail.
- *Playgrounds:* There are 2 dry playgrounds and a wet playground that includes water cannons and splashing fun located near the leisure pools at the tree house area of the resort.
- *Other activities.* Tennis, basketball, golf, bike rentals, and bass fishing excursions.

Amy's Analysis. If you are looking for a quieter, not as "Disney" place to unwind when you are in the parks, this resort is a solid option. It is also great for large groups and families looking for extra quiet spaces (think tree houses).

Old Key West Resort

Accessible ★★★★ Quiet ★★★ Convenient ★★★ Overall ★★★

Just as the name implies, there is a beachy feel that suggests relaxation is the theme of your vacation. The villas are great; they have everything you need to be away from it all.

Rooms. All of the rooms are suites with a kitchen, living area, and a variety of bedrooms. Some of the rooms are in the main resort area that has several buildings in a colony with a central building containing the lobby, restaurants, and gift shop. This resort is spread out. If you would like to be near the pool or lobby, request proximity to the Hospitality House.

Amenities include:

- Free Wi-Fi
- Hair dryer
- Coffee maker

- Phone with voice mail
- Small in-room safe
- Full-size refrigerator
- Microwave
- Toaster
- Cooking and eating utensils, pans, plates, etc.
- Washer and dryer (except in studio rooms)
- Ironing board/iron
- Pack 'n' play ask at desk
- USB ports and outlets on nightstand
- H20 brand shampoo, conditioner, shower gel, lotion and facial soap, and bar soap for the sink

The accessible rooms have a variety of options. Some include hearing accessibility, some have a roll-in shower, others have tubs with bars. Not all of the rooms have ADA-recommended heights for dressers, tables, and countertops. Most rooms have 2 queen beds, but all of the rooms with the roll-in shower option have 1 king bed.

You are able to choose a room online with the accommodations that work best for your family. When you click on "room rates," options for different rooms come up. Click the little box that says "accessible rooms." If you are more comfortable speaking with a Disney cast member, call reservations at (407) 939-5277 and explain which accommodations you need.

Transportation. There are buses for all parks, and a boat or quick walk to Disney Springs.

Dining. Although it appears the dining is limited, keep in mind that every room has a kitchen, and you are a quick boat ride to Disney Springs where there are many dining options. But, if you want some convenience in dining, I would look at a different resort. There are no counter-service options that are not a poolside snack bar.

- *Olivia's Café.* $$, table service.
- *Gurgling Suitcase Libations and Spirits.* $, pool bar, lunch and dinner
- *Good's Food to Go.* $, counter service, breakfast, lunch, and dinner.
- *Turtle Shack Snacks.* $, counter service, breakfast, lunch, and dinner.

Recreation. Recreation options include:

- *Pools.* The sandcastle slide and sauna disguised as a lighthouse create a charming main pool area. There is a lift for a wheelchair and a sandy area that includes a playground on one side of the pool. There are also

3 leisure pools where loud play and splashing are "gently discouraged." All three have playgrounds nearby, though there is a large amount of sand surrounding them.

- *Arcades.* Classic and modern arcade games and air hockey. A Florida law prohibits games that dispense tickets for prizes.
- *Movies under the stars.* Watch Disney movies outside under the stars. There's a schedule for movies near the pool and at the concierge desk.
- *Campfire.* Come listen to campfire stories and roast marshmallows.
- *Jogging trail.* Marked, paved jogging trail.
- *Other activities.* Tennis, basketball, golf, bike rentals, bass fishing excursions, playgrounds.

Amy's Analysis. If you have a family member with sensory needs, I would be aware of the lack of dining choices, and of all the sand. If there are no issues with sand, Old Key West is a nice option that feels like a beach get-away. There are fully equipped villas with a washer and dryer in most rooms, and Disney Springs is close for dining options.

Moderate Resorts

There are five resorts that are considered to be moderate. They have nice rooms, great pools, good amenities, and all of the benefits included in staying at a Disney resort.

Best value. All of them are fairly equal in amenities and room rates.

Amy's pick. This one is a tie. It really all boils down to the pool. If you will spend a lot of time at the resort pool, I would choose the Caribbean. There is zero entry, a great water play area, nice bar, and an overall better set up. If you won't be at the pool much, then I recommend Port Orleans: French Quarter. It is smaller, easier to navigate, and only has one bus stop.

Disney's Caribbean Resort

Accessible ★★★★ Quiet ★★★ Convenient ★★★ Overall ★★★

Note: There is a lot of construction at this resort. Old Port Royale is closed, so gift shops, eating, and the pool bar area are all impacted and are currently housed in trucks and a large, air-conditioned tent. The construction affects much of the resort and its surrounding area making it impossible to avoid. Until 2019 I suggest choosing a different resort.

Get away to a beautiful island retreat with beautifully colored villages. Old Port Royale is the main building with the food court, information desk, arcade, and gift shop.

Rooms. Nice-sized rooms, most with 2 queen beds and a small table with 2 chairs. Decorated with a Nemo decor. The bathrooms are split (2 sinks and a dressing area are separated from the shower and toilet) with nice counter space and shelving for storage. The towels and toiletries are nice quality.

Some of the rooms have a pirate theme. Well decorated with ships for beds and cool touches everywhere, but they are pretty far from Old Port Royale. There is a bus stop and a leisure pool nearby. But considering the location and the extra cost for a themed room, it is not a good value.

I used to recommend the Martinique Village area of the resort, but it happens to be right in the heart of the construction.

Amenities include:

- Free Wi-Fi
- Hair dryer
- Coffee maker
- Phone with voice mail
- Small in-room safe
- Small refrigerator
- Ironing board/iron
- Pack 'n' play
- USB ports and outlets on nightstand
- H20 brand shampoo, conditioner & facial soap

The accessible rooms have a variety of options. Some include hearing accessibility, some have a roll-in shower, others have tubs with bars. Not all of the rooms have ADA-recommended heights for dressers, tables, and countertops. Most rooms have 2 queen beds, but all of the rooms with the roll-in shower option have 1 king bed.

You are able to choose a room online with the accommodations that work best for your family. When you click on "room rates," options for different rooms come up. Click the little box that says "accessible rooms." If you are more comfortable speaking with a Disney cast member, call reservations at (407) 939-5277 and explain which accommodations you need.

Transportation. There are buses for all parks.

Dining. The dining is currently in a food truck by the main pool, an air-conditioned tent with a buffet, and three rooms re-designed to be snack bars. The pool bar is also a trailer.

Recreation. Recreation options include:

- *Pools.* Decorated as a colonial Spanish fortress with water slides and water cannons, zero entry, and shipwreck themed water play area, my family loves this pool. The layout is generous, it has a bar, and a sandy beach to play on or easily avoid. There are six leisure pools, one in every village. There are lifts for wheelchairs and splashing and loud play are "gently discouraged."

- *Arcade.* Classic and modern arcade games and air hockey. A Florida law prohibits games that dispense tickets for prizes. (Closed during construction.)
- *Movies under the stars.* Watch Disney movies outside under the stars. There's a schedule for movies near the pool and at the concierge desk.
- *Campfire.* Come listen to campfire stories and roast marshmallows.
- *Jogging trail.* Marked, paved jogging trail. (Closed during construction.)
- Other activities (subject to construction closures). Volleyball, bike rentals, playground.

Amy's Analysis. If you happen to find a deal you can't refuse and choose to stay at the Caribbean Beach during construction, there are a few benefits. Most of the rooms now have a small day (for a young child) bed allowing five guests to have a bed. A special pin set, featuring the Three Caballeros in construction outfits, is a free gift with the room and there is special entertainment including live bands and character visits at the main pool.

Coronado Springs

Accessible ★★ Quiet ★★ Convenient ★★ Overall ★★

Note: Coronado Springs is undergoing construction. They are adding a 15-foot tower near the central building. Unlike the construction at the Caribbean, this is focused in one area and does little to interrupt your stay.

A resort and convention center with Southwest theming. The layout is similar to the Caribbean Beach, with a central building and other groups of buildings with guest rooms surrounding the lake. The resort is very large and spread out, and there are often more business travelers than tourists. The convention center function of the resort lends itself to having club-level rooms and amenities at a more moderate rate (although still pricey).

Rooms. Nice-sized rooms, most with 2 queen beds, and a small table with 2 chairs. Decorated with a desert or Southwest décor. The bathrooms are split (1 sink and a dressing area are separated from the shower and toilet) with nice counter space and shelving for storage. The towels and toiletries are nice quality. There aren't balconies at moderate resorts, so my family doesn't choose to upgrade our view.

There is a grouping of rooms that are considered preferred. These are closer to El Centro (main lobby building) and the main pool. The preferred rate is higher, but in a resort this spread out, I recommend it if your budget allows.

Amenities include:

- Free Wi-Fi
- Hair dryer
- Coffee maker
- Phone with voice mail
- Small in-room safe
- Small refrigerator
- Ironing board/iron
- Pack 'n' play
- USB ports and outlets on nightstand
- H20 brand shampoo, conditioner & facial soap

The accessible rooms have a variety of options. Some include hearing accessibility, some have a roll-in shower, others have tubs with bars. Not all of the rooms have ADA-recommended heights for dressers, tables, and countertops. Most rooms have 2 queen beds, but all of the rooms with the roll-in shower option have 1 king bed.

You are able to choose a room online with the accommodations that work best for your family. When you click on "room rates," options for different rooms come up. Click the little box that says "accessible rooms." If you are more comfortable speaking with a Disney cast member, call reservations at (407) 939-5277 and explain which accommodations you need.

Transportation. There are buses for all parks.

Dining. The dining options aren't plentiful, but they work well for families. All the moderates also have a food court and pool bars.

- *Maya Grill.* $-$$ table service, breakfast, lunch, and dinner.

Recreation. Recreation options include:

- *Pools.* A Mayan temple looks over the main pool, which has a water slide. There is a shallow pool with splashing fountains. Behind the temple is a fun playground area and dig site (yes, it involves sand). Wheelchairs enter using a lift. There are also 3 leisure pools where splashing and loud play are "gently discouraged."
- *Arcade.* Classic and modern arcade games and air hockey. A Florida law prohibits games that dispense tickets for prizes.
- *Movies under the stars.* Watch Disney movies outside under the stars. There's a schedule for movies near the pool and at the concierge desk.

- *Campfire.* Come listen to campfire stories and roast marshmallows.
- *Jogging trail.* Marked, paved jogging trail.
- *Playground.* There is a cool playground and dig site; of course this includes sand, but also a firm spongy floor.
- *Other activities.* Volleyball, fitness room.

Amy's Analysis. The Coronado is my least favorite of the moderate resorts. Its size is the biggest issue; it's so large that even a walk to El Centro can take a typical walker 15 minutes.

Disney's Port Orleans: Riverside

Accessible ★★★ Quiet ★★★ Convenient ★★★ Overall ★★★

Stroll on down for some Southern hospitality with Louisiana's bayous and sprawling mansions. The Riverside Mill is the central building with the lobby, food court, arcade, and gift shop, then there are two themes: the rural south (Alligator Bayou) and the plantation-style mansions (Magnolia Bend). This is a pet friendly resort accepting up to 2 pet dogs per room for an additional $50/night fee.

Rooms. Magnolia Bend has 3-story buildings resembling the mansions form the southern plantations. Alligator Bayou is very rustic and not as simple to navigate. All of the amenities are the same, the one difference being Alligator Bayou rooms also include a Murphy bed for a 5th person (probably best for a child). Nice-sized rooms, most with 2 queen beds, and a small table with 2 chairs. The bathrooms are split (2 sinks and a dressing area are separated from the shower and toilet) with nice counter space and shelving for storage. The towels and toiletries are good quality. There aren't balconies at moderate resorts, so my family doesn't choose to upgrade our view.

Some of the rooms (called Royal Rooms) in Magnolia Bend have a princess theme. Well decorated with dark blue and gold, so no need to worry about an explosion of pink and glitter. They are very well themed with touches that represent most of the princesses before *Frozen*. They are naturally more expensive. I don't believe any of the Royal Rooms are accessible.

It is pretty dark and natural looking in the Alligator Bayou. I know full-grown adults who have gotten the willies at night walking back to their room, and it's easy to get lost there.

Amenities include:

- Free Wi-Fi
- Hair dryer
- Coffee maker
- Phone with voice mail

- Small in-room safe
- Small refrigerator
- Ironing board/iron
- Pack 'n' play
- USB ports and outlets on nightstand
- H20 brand shampoo, conditioner & facial soap

The accessible rooms have a variety of options. Some include hearing accessibility, some have a roll-in shower, others have tubs with bars. Not all of the rooms have ADA-recommended heights for dressers, tables, and countertops. Most rooms have 2 queen beds, but all of the rooms with the roll-in shower option have 1 king bed.

You are able to choose a room online with the accommodations that work best for your family. When you click on "room rates," options for different rooms come up. Click the little box that says "accessible rooms." If you are more comfortable speaking with a Disney cast member, call reservations at (407) 939-5277 and explain which accommodations you need.

Transportation. There are buses for all parks and a boat to Disney Springs. Our experience with the buses was not good. I know improvements were made for timing, but I don't love the bus stop locations for the Alligator Bayou area.

Dining. The dining options aren't plentiful, but they work well for families. All the moderates also have a food court and pool bars.

- *Boatwright's Dining Hall.* $$, table service, dinner only.

Recreation. Recreation options include:

- *Pools.* The swimming hole has a water slide and water play area. A chair lift provides access to the pool for wheelchairs. There are five leisure pools, three in Alligator Bayou and two in Magnolia Bend. Splashing and loud play are "gently discouraged."
- *Arcade.* Classic and modern arcade games and air hockey. A Florida law prohibits games that dispense tickets for prizes.
- *Movies under the stars.* Watch Disney movies outside under the stars. There's a schedule for movies near the pool and at the concierge desk.
- *Campfire.* Come listen to campfire stories and roast marshmallows.
- *Jogging trail.* Marked, paved jogging trail.
- Other activities. Bike rentals, bass fishing excursions, playground, horse-drawn carriage rides (for a fee).

Amy's Analysis. If you are traveling when it is less crowded, you are likely to get the area you request. However, no request is guaranteed, so if you prefer one area to another, I would not choose this resort. The pet policy can be something to consider for your family.

Disney's Port Orleans: French Quarter

Accessible ★★★ Quiet ★★★ Convenient ★★★ Overall ★★★

There is always a great time to be had in the French Quarter. Of course, this is Disney, and there are some obvious differences in this inspiration. This is a quaint, quiet resort. There are far fewer rooms and buildings, and only one bus stop. As long as the pool isn't a big focus, you can be very happy here.

Rooms. The buildings all have rod-iron railings with a New Orleans feel and none of them are very far from the main building. Nice-sized rooms, most with 2 queen beds, and a small table with 2 chairs. The bathrooms are split (2 sinks and a dressing area are separated from the shower and toilet) with good counter space and shelving for storage. The towels and toiletries are nice quality. There aren't balconies at moderate resorts, so my family doesn't choose to upgrade our view.

Amenities include:

- Free Wi-Fi
- Hair dryer
- Coffee maker
- Phone with voice mail
- Small in-room safe
- Small refrigerator
- Ironing board/iron
- Pack 'n' play
- USB ports and outlets on nightstand
- H20 brand shampoo, conditioner & facial soap

The accessible rooms have a variety of options. Some include hearing accessibility, some have a roll-in shower, others have tubs with bars. Not all of the rooms have ADA-recommended heights for dressers, tables, and countertops. Most rooms have 2 queen beds, but all of the rooms with the roll-in shower option have 1 king bed.

You are able to choose a room online with the accommodations that work best for your family. When you click on "room rates," options for different rooms come up. Click the little box that says "accessible rooms." If you are more comfortable speaking with a Disney cast member, call reservations at (407) 939-5277 and explain which accommodations you need.

Transportation. There are buses for all parks, and a boat to Disney Springs.

Dining. The dining option is just a food court. There are no table-service restaurants here, though Port Orleans: Riverside (with its Boatwright's Dining Hall) is a short walk away.

Recreation. Recreation options include:

- *Pools.* King Neptune is watching over all of the fun with a sea serpent slide and alligator jazz musicians that squirt water. There's also a water play and a poolside bar. A chair lift provides access to the pool for wheelchairs. There are no leisure pools, and in general the pool area like the rest of the resort is on a smaller scale.
- *Arcade.* Classic and modern arcade games and air hockey. A Florida law prohibits games that dispense tickets for prizes.
- *Movies under the stars.* Watch Disney movies outside under the stars. There's a schedule for movies near the pool and at the concierge desk.
- *Campfire.* Come listen to campfire stories and roast marshmallows.
- *Jogging trail.* Marked, paved jogging trail.
- *Other activities.* Bike rentals, bass fishing excursions, playground, horse-drawn carriage rides (for a fee).

Amy's Analysis. This is truly a lovely resort. The smaller scale is great for a lot of reasons, though if you want a bigger, better pool, you'll want to look into other options.

Fort Wilderness Cabins

Accessible ★★ Quiet ★★★★ Convenient ★★ Overall ★★★

If your family enjoys camping with all of the conveniences of home (toilets, beds, air conditioning, and TV), this is the location for you. Cabins are a great way to have suite-style accommodations at a moderate price; however, the transportation is more complicated. This is a pet friendly resort accepting up to 2 pet dogs per room for an additional $50/night fee.

Rooms. All of the rooms are individual cabins. There is a living area with a queen sized sleeper sofa, chairs, table, and a TV. The kitchen has a full-sized refrigerator and ice-maker, 2-burner stove, a combination microwave/convection oven, toaster, and all of the pans and other kitchen tools you'll need. The bedroom has a queen sized bed and a bunk bed. And even though you are camping, there's a bathroom, too.

There are accessible cabins with ramps and hearing-accessible rooms with visual alarms and doorbells. You are able to choose a room online with the accommodations that work best for your family. When you click on "room rates," options for different rooms come up. Click the little box that says "accessible rooms." If you are more comfortable speaking with a Disney cast member, call reservations at (407) 939-5277 and explain which accommodations you need.

Amenities include:

- Free Wi-Fi
- Hair dryer
- Coffee maker
- Phone with voice mail
- Small in-room safe
- Small refrigerator
- Ironing board/iron
- Pack 'n' play
- USB ports and outlets on nightstand
- H20 brand shampoo, conditioner & facial soap

Transportation. There is an internal bus that circles to pick guests up and take them to the main bus stop where a transfer is required to get on the bus (or boat for the Magic Kingdom). If you have a car, it will be much easier and faster to drive yourself. Every cabin has its own parking space, and parking is free at all parks and throughout the resort for guests.

Dining. If you consider the cabins camping, you'll be very surprised to hear there is a range of options for dining.

- *Trails End.* $$ table service, breakfast, brunch, and dinner.
- *P&J's Takeout.* $, counter service, breakfast, lunch, and dinner.
- *Meadows Pool Bar.* $, drinks, light menu, snacks.
- *Crockett's Tavern.* $, lounge.
- *Hoop-Dee-Doo Musical Review.* $$$$, vaudeville-style stage show with a country theme that does not include Disney characters.
- *Mickey's Backyard BBQ.* $$$$, hoedown dinner buffet with Mickey and friends.

Recreation. Recreation options include:

- *Pools.* The Meadows pool has the activities and a corkscrew slide. There is a leisure pool where splashing and loud play are "gently discouraged". Both pools use a lift for wheelchair accessibility.
- *Campfire.* Come listen to campfire stories and roast marshmallows. with Chip and Dale.
- 2 Arcades Classic and modern arcade games and air hockey. A Florida

law prohibits games that dispense tickets for prizes.

- *Movies under the stars.* Watch Disney movies outside under the stars. There's a schedule for movies near the pool and at the concierge desk.
- *Jogging trail. Marked, paved jogging trail.*
- *Other activities.* Basketball, volleyball.
- *Other activities with an extra fee.* Archery classes with instructors, pony rides, wagon rides, boat rentals, guided fishing tours, canoe and kayak rentals, bike rentals, Segway tour.

Amy's Analysis. If camping is what your family loves, this is a fabulous place to be. Even if your family has never considered camping, but want more space and a quiet area at a better rate (especially if you have a car with you), then Fort Wilderness is a great pick.

Value Resorts

Value resorts are a less expensive way to have access to all of the benefits of staying on property. They are not plush or super comfortable (the bus lines are in queues, not a friendly bench with shelter). The amenities are fewer and even the toilet paper and towels are an inferior quality. They are also smaller and noisy. The walls are thin, and often there are large teams or groups of kids that are not worried about their noise levels.

Of course the rooms meet ADA requirements and an electric cart will fit in the room to charge; however, think minimums. Space is tight.

It's not all bad: the rooms are clean, the staff is great, and families love the huge statues and Disney fun throughout these resorts.

Disney's Art of Animation

This is a pet friendly resort accepting up to 2 pet dogs per room for an additional $50/night fee.

- Themes: Cars, Finding Nemo, Lion King and Little Mermaid.
- The suites have 1 queen bed, 1 double table bed, 1 double sleeper sofa (they will sleep 6 adults, but they are not as big as you might expect).
- The Finding Nemo pool is zero entry and plays music underwater. This is the pool where you will find organized activities.
- The other areas each have a pool, splash pad, and a lift for accessibility.

Pop Century

- Themes: 50s, 60s, 70s, and 80s, with statues and large toys from each decade.
- Considered the most interesting of the value resorts.

All Star Sports

- Sports theme.
- Very popular with sports teams that come for tournaments at the Wide World of Sports.

All Star Music

- Music theme.
- There are a few family suites with 1 queen bed, 1 double-size sleeper sofa, a twin-size sleeper chair, and a twin-size sleeper ottoman.
- The Calypso Pool is a guitar-shaped with a large fountain in the middle featuring the Three Caballeros.

All Star Movies

- Movie theme.
- The Fantasia Pool has a fountain featuring Sorcerer Mickey that lightly sprays swimmers passing by.

Rooms. The buildings all have rod iron railings and none of them are very far from the main building. Nice-sized rooms, most have 2 queen beds and a small table with 2 chairs. The bathrooms are split (2 sinks and a dressing area are separated from the shower and toilet) with nice counter space and shelving for storage. The towels and toiletries are nice quality. There aren't balconies at value resorts, so my family doesn't choose to upgrade our view.

Amenities include:

- Free Wi-Fi
- Hair dryer
- Iron/ ironing board
- Phone with voice mail
- Small in-room safe
- Mini refrigerator
- Ironing board/iron
- H20 brand shampoo, conditioner combined and bar soap

The accessible rooms have a variety of options. Some include hearing accessibility, some have a roll-in shower, others have tubs with bars. Not all of the rooms have ADA-recommended heights for dressers, tables, and countertops. Most rooms have 2 queen beds, but all of the rooms with the roll-in shower option have 1 king bed.

You are able to choose a room online with the accommodations that work best for your family. When you click on "room rates," options for different rooms come up. Click the little box that says "accessible rooms." If you are more comfortable speaking with a Disney cast member, call reservations at (407) 939-5277 and explain which accommodations you need.

Transportation. There are buses to take you to all parks and Disney Springs.

Dining. Dining options are limited to food courts and pool bars.

Recreation. Recreation options include:

- *Pools. Each of the Values has its own themed pool.*
- *Arcade.* Classic and modern arcade games and air hockey. A Florida law prohibits games that dispense tickets for prizes.
- *Movies under the stars.* Watch Disney movies outside under the stars on select nights. There's a schedule for movies near the pool and at the concierge desk.
- *Jogging trail.* Marked, paved jogging trail.
- *Other activities.* Surrey bike rentals and playground.

Amy's Analysis. The Value resorts are well named. You benefit from all of the on-property perks, at a cost that may work better for your budget. If you are able to stretch that budget a bit, however, I recommend a moderate resort.

CHAPTER FIVE

Tickets and Reservations

There are probably more reservations involved in a Walt Disney World vacation than anywhere else you need, but with a little planning it all makes the vacation much easier.

My Disney Experience and My Magic Plus. Of course Disney has an "app for that." And even if you don't use a smart phone, this step is important (and can be done on a computer with a real keyboard). Every reservation will be synced on your MyDisneyExperience account, so you will need one.

Download the app on your phone or go to disneyworld.disney.go.com and select the tab "My Disney Experience," then follow the prompts to create an account. You need accounts for everyone traveling with you, including young children and guests without phones.

You will use this account for all of your reservations and tickets (even if you have military or outside vendor tickets).

Once you have everyone's accounts ready you can make reservations.

Resort Reservations. After you have researched all of your options, it's time to book your room. You really can't do this too early. Having a room allows you to book dinner reservations and FastPasses earlier than guests just visiting the parks.

You have two choices in making reservations: online (disneyworld.disney.go.com) or on the phone (407) 939-5277. This is all about personal preference.

If you need special accommodations, I prefer the phone; just to make sure you can ask questions and be sure of what you need. But if it is 1 am and the phone isn't an option, click the "accommodation" button on the web site and you will see all of the options.

Dining Reservations. There are many options for dining. At 180 days before your vacation, at 6am EST, you can make dining reservations. If you have resort reservations, then you may make reservations for your whole vacation at one time. If you are staying off property you will need to make reservations each morning at 180 days out.

For example, if you make a reservation on Monday for a date 180 days from now, on Tuesday you will need to log in or call for the next day's reservations (this is a perk of staying on property; you get a head start and it is more convenient).

You may call (407)939-5277 or make reservations online. This is a case where online is faster and possibly more effective for the big reservations than using an operator. If you want to dine at popular locations during busy times, you must make your reservations as early and as quickliy as you can. Be flexible about dates and don't discount other possibilities.

FastPasses (FP+). A FastPass is a reservation for an attraction at Walt Disney World. There are two lines for most attractions, one for guests with FP+ and one for those without.

The new MyMagicPlus (MM+) system allows you to make FastPasses 60 or 30 days ahead of your trip depending on where you are staying. You no longer have to be at rope drop and run for Toy Story Mania or Space Mountain only to be given FastPass with a redemption time 5 hours later. Now you use your phone or computer to make a more convenient reservations (however, the choices with the most popular attractions are limited).

To use the FP+, come back to the attraction during the time listed on your app (or printout of your computer screen) with your ticket or MagicBand and enter the FastPass return line. You will scan your ticket or MagicBand on a glowing Mickey like you do at the main gate, and then go on in. You will notice the line is much faster than the stand-by line.

FP+ rules:

- You have to have tickets purchased and entered in your account.
- You may only make 3 FP+ per day in a single park before your trip. For example, on Monday 3 for Magic Kingdom, Tuesday 3 for Epcot, Wednesday 3 for Animal Kingdom, etc.
- Epcot and Hollywood Studios have a tier system that makes you choose from certain categories For example, at Epcot you can't have FP+ for Test Track, Soarin', and Frozen Ever After. Those are really the only 3 FP+ anyone really wants in Epcot, so they make you choose. The idea is you can have a quick line, then wait in a longer one.
- After you have used the FPs+ reserved for that day, you may make one more from your phone, as many times as you would like, and it can be for another park. There probably won't be one available for Frozen Ever After, or Seven Dwarfs Mine Train on the same day, but a lot of attractions will still have openings.
- I suggest making early FPs+ so you can continue to make more throughout the day.

- If you qualify for a DAS (Disability Access Services) pass, you may have both without conflict, and a DAS pass does not have an end time that cancels it.

Tickets. Disney has several choices for tickets.

- *One-Day, One-Park Pass.* You can visit one park only that day. You may leave and come back to that park, but no other park.
- *One-Day Park Hopper.* You may visit all four parks on your single day.
- *Multi-Day Pass.* This pass allows you to go to one park a day for however many days you paid for. Example: Monday, Magic Kingdom; Tuesday, Epcot; Wednesday, Magic Kingdom; etc. You may visit any of the four main parks, but only the same park each day, for example, morning at Animal Kingdom, back to the room to break, back to Animal Kingdom.
- *Multi Day with Park Hopper.* You may go to any of the four main parks any time you like for as many days as you purchased. Example: Monday morning, Magic Kingdom, then Disney's Hollywood Studios; Tuesday, Epcot, then Animal Kingdom; etc.
- *Multi Day with Park Hopper and More.* Like the multi-day Park Hoppers, but they include water parks and other activities.

I highly suggest upgrading to the Park Hopper. When we go, my family likes to break it up, but the biggest reason for the Park Hopper is being able to go back to visit favorite rides. If you are traveling with someone with a developmental disability, they can easily fixate on a certain ride. My son loves Toy Story Mania at Disney's Hollywood Studios. He needs to be able to get back to that ride in order to enjoy the rest of the vacation. If you can only do one park a day, it greatly affects your flexibility.

If you do not plan on going to the water parks, I do not recommend the "and More" option.

You can order tickets as a part of your resort package at wwww.waltdisneyworld.disney.go.com or on the phone (407) 939-5277. For military tickets, the family member in the military must visit their tickets and travel office on base. (Don't wait to purchase them at Shades of Green because you need them to schedule Fast Passes.)

There are very few discounts on tickets. Do not trust most of what you see.

MagicBands. A MagicBand is your room key, tickets, FP+ reservations, charge card (if you want it to be), and Disney Dining tool all in one. If you are a guest in the resorts, they are complimentary and will be mailed to your home before you leave. Don't forget to personalize them on your MyDisneyExperience account first.

MagicBands arrive as a one-size-fits-most bracelets. They are a clever design that allows for a wide range of sizes. Knowing not everyone wants to wear a bracelet, the new design (as of winter 2017) has a removable disk that can fit in a lanyard purchased separately.

If you do not want a MagicBand, you may ask for a traditional plastic card-style key and ticket.

CHAPTER SIX

Timelines and Packing Lists

If you miss a day or you're behind, your vacation isn't ruined. These recommendations will help:

Timeline

- Create a MyDisneyExperience account (and download the app if you have a smart phone).
- Pick a date.
- Make hotel reservations even if you are staying off property, and write down your confirmation number (write it down even if you have it stored in your email or on your phone).
- Decide on a game plan: what parks you are visiting, what kind of dining you will do, what days you would like to be in which parks.
- At 180 days out, and exactly at 9am EST, make dinner reservations. Write down that date and put it somewhere you'll see it every day so you won't forget to call or go online when it's time.
- If tickets weren't purchased when you booked a room, buy tickets.
- If you bought tickets from someplace other than Disney, enter ticket numbers into your MyDisneyExperience account, and write them down as well.
- If you are flying, start looking at flights.
- If you have a flight and want to use Magical Express, call (407) 939-5277 to give them your flight info. they will set up Magical Express.
- Rent any strollers or electric carts you will need.
- At 60 days out make FastPass+ reservations at 7:00am EST. Write down that date and put it somewhere you'll see it every day so you won't forget to call or go online when it's time.

- If you are not staying on property, 30 days out Make FastPass+ reservations at 7:00am EST. Write down that date and put it somewhere you'll see it every day so you won't forget to call or go online when it's time.
- Arrange for pet care.
- If flying with a service animal or emotional support animal, get all paperwork ordered and ready before you call the airlines.
- If staying at a Disney resort, check in online using your MyDisneyExperience account. You can do this as early as 30 days ahead.
- Stop papers and mail (or have a neighbor pick them up). Can someone take out the garbage that week?
- Pack.
- Travel.

Of course you also need to front-load and work with everyone about expectations and what to do on a schedule that works for your family (some families think it's best to surprise the kids).

Packing

When you are packing for the vacation, remember all of the little things that make your family comfortable. Include snack items, weighted blankets, corn silk brushes, or other occupational therapy items. Most importantly, include the favorite pillow, stuffed animal, or blanket.

Lockers are reasonably priced at WDW. You can stash some of your larger items (including a soft cooler with familiar snacks) that you may need in an emergency for $10 large, $8 small. Not bad for peace of mind.

Packing is a very individual thing. Much of it depends on how you are traveling and of course each family needs different things. You'll find my complete packing list in the appendix, and there is also a printable list on my website.

CHAPTER SEVEN

Your Own Fairy Godmother (or Father)

We have discussed when to travel, how to work the budget, tickets, and resorts; now I'm going to let you in on a great secret. There are professionals able to put it all together for you, and *it's free.* Travel agents can book your vacation for almost everything you will be doing in Walt Disney World—your rooms, tickets, meals, FastPasses—and they get you the best value possible. As certified travel agents, they are paid by Disney.

When you contact a travel agent they will ask a few questions, like when you want to travel, how many are traveling with you, have you ever been to a Disney property before, and of course your budget. If you have already decided a few things, or even most things, they will take all of that information and provide you with some quotes. If you are within six months of your travel date, they will offer to make dining reservations right away, or be ready to book those reservations at your 180-day mark. They will make sure you have everyone set up for My Disney Experience and walk you through downloading the app if you aren't tech savvy. Closer to the vacation date they will talk with you about which attractions you want FastPasses for, and at 7:00am 60 days from your vacation they will be up and on their computers booking those FastPasses for you.

I enjoy planning a Disney vacation, so I hadn't felt a need to look into a travel agent before, but for the sake of research we used one on our last trip. I had looked at the resorts we might want and knew when we were traveling, but I hadn't gotten the ball rolling yet. Then an ad popped up on Facebook with the summer discount rates for resorts. I called my agent immediately and she started looking for the best rates. Because of the discounts, she was able to upgrade us into Deluxe for only $50 more a night than the moderate we were looking at. We made a decision, and she booked us at the Animal Kingdom Lodge. Then, as we got closer to our vacation, we discussed FastPasses. Pandora had not opened yet at Animal Kingdom, but we knew we needed to book Pandora first thing, so she was ready. I'll admit, leaving that in someone else's hands felt a little uncomfortable, but it was meant to be. Our FastPass+ reservation date was right in the middle of my daughter's graduation and prepping Cincinnati's Autism Walk. I had an important appointment and there was no way I could have booked those FastPasses. I received a text from my agent that it was all done, and we had everything we wanted. I was so happy that everything didn't depend on me this time, it felt like I had a Fairy Godmother.

Here are some reasons why you should use a travel agent:

- They can wait on hold for you. When the hurricanes come, the agents spend six hours or more on hold to adjust their clients' vacations and make sure everything is correct.
- When new specials are announced, they contact Disney to see how your vacation can benefit from the new prices.
- You have a Disney expert ready to answer any questions for you; even if you are in the park, you can just call them.
- Some agencies have incentives, for example, mine gives custom embroidered bags to the kids, or a Disney gift card.
- If you use a Disney-certified travel agent, it's free.

There are agencies out there that do not follow all of Disney's best practices. If you see any of these things, look for another agent.

- They charge you to book dining or FastPass+.
- The price is too high or too good to be true.
- You contact them and you don't hear back quickly.
- They try to up-sell you. Some recommendations are great, but a good agent will know the Disney Dining Plan is typically not the best use of your budget, and they will explain the pros and cons.

My travel agent, Leslie Sawhook at Exclusive Travel Partners, has her masters in special education and taught it for many years. Other agents on her team are parents of children with special needs. I recommend Exclusive Travel Partners, and Leslie in particular.

There are so many things to plan and prepare as you get ready for a Disney vacation, why not let a "fairy godparent" help you create some of the magic.

CHAPTER EIGHT

Disney's Extra Special Service

The most significant thing that separates Disney theme parks from any other park is their customer service. Companies around the world try to imitate the Disney training programs, but Disney sets the standard. This means Disney has every reason to want your family and every one of their guests to be as comfortable as possible. They do understand that many of guests have needs that may differ from the average guest, and they have policies to meet those needs to the best of their ability.

Preparing for a Vacation with Special Needs

For every family, planning a Disney vacation preparation is important. There are a few specific things you and your family can do to be as ready as you can for this adventure:

YouTube. Many people have an easier time with new adventures if some of the mystery is uncovered. There are many videos on YouTube that show the parks, attractions, and characters. Share them with your family so they have a better idea of what to expect. In most cases, Disney has not approved these clips, so watch out for inappropriate language or behavior.

Go for Walks. There is a lot of walking at WDW. As you plan for your vacation, take walks around your neighborhood or a park and gradually make your walks a little longer to get your family's legs ready.

Disney's Policies for Special Needs

There are some specific policies Disney uses in guiding their cast members on how to help guests with special needs. Many of the policies are universal to most public places concerning physical disabilities; of course, Disney is fully ADA compliant, but they separate themselves from the pack by

not obvious to the public. Whether
od allergy, Disney goes beyond the
ortable and safe.

e (DAS)

a non-visible or developmental disability
, seizure disorder, medical concerns, and
prevent them from enjoying an attraction
tion, DAS can help you. If you have a mobil-
it, ental disability, then you do not need a DAS.

- Go t at any of the 4 major parks with all members of your grou
- Ask politely for a DAS.
- You will be asked why you need one. Explain which accommodations you need and why. You don't have to share a diagnosis, and cast members aren't allowed to ask, but if you are comfortable sharing this information, it is helpful.
- If it is decided that you qualify for a DAS, the system will be explained to you. You will be shown an iPad with the policies in really small print. Basically, it's meant to inform you that you that having a DAS doesn't give you immediate access to anything.
- The guest that requires the DAS will have their MagicBand or park ticket scanned, then their photo will be taken in a very casual way—no posing or smiling required.
- Next, the cast member scans the MagicBand or park ticket of every guest visiting with them. This enters you in the system as a guest that can enter attractions with the DAS holder.
- Now you are free to enjoy the parks. The pass is good for 90 days, after which it must be renewed.
- Once you have a DAS and are in the parks:
- Approach a cast member at the attraction you would like to ride. Ask for a DAS return time. The cast member will scan your band or ticket, ask who is riding, then verbally give you a return time. You can see it on your MyDisneyExperience app. Anyone registered with the DAS can do this. The guest with the disability does not have to be there for this step.
- Go and enjoy another attraction, eat, spend time in a sensory spot (like a playground or Tom Sawyer Island), do some shopping, or whatever you want to do to pass the time in a way that suits your family.

- At the designated time (which will be 10 minutes less than the posted standby time; for example, if the wait for Seven Dwarfs Mine Train is 75 minutes long at 1:00pm, then the return time will be 2:05), come to the FastPass line for the attraction. The guest with the DAS *must ride.*
- The guest with the DAS enters the line first for your group and touches their MagicBand or ticket to the glowing Mickey light.
- The light will turn blue (don't panic!). The blue light allows the cast member to see the photo on their screen. Then the light will turn green and all of you may enter as if you had regular FastPasses.

Troubleshooting

DAS is a big issue of concern for many families. Here are some of the more frequently asked questions:

- If I have multiple family members that need a DAS, can they still each have one, and can we all be registered to each pass? Yes, your family will be registered for each pass, but no guest may have more than one DAS reservation at a time. For example, Dad will be with child #1 on Space Mountain and Mom is with child #2 at Peter Pan.
- What if the system breaks down? When the technology isn't cooperating, they resort to paper. A paper pass is given with the return time and number of guests that will be riding.
- What if my child won't wear the MagicBand? No worries, someone else can have the band as long as the guest the DAS was issued to is there when entering the FastPass queue.
- The policy reads that only 6 may enter the ride on a DAS. What if there are more than 6 of us? Bring *everyone* to guest services. All of them will be registered to the DAS. Then your family can decide who rides what (ask guest services about the 6 person limit; large groups can be accommodated under special circumstances).

Some tips for DAS users:

- Have FastPasses scheduled before your arrival. My son, Ben, was able to ride Toy Story Mania (a popular ride) 3 times one morning: first because of magic hours, so the line was very short, then with a DAS reservation, then right before we left he had a FastPass we had set up 60 days prior.
- Have the guest with the DAS enter first. This allows the return process to be very quick and inconspicuous.
- Be late by at least a minute. There isn't a grace period to start (although there is no end time). Sometimes the FastPass clocks can be off by a few seconds, and you want to be sure the system is ready for you.

- Always keep your cool and be nice. If something isn't working the way you expect it to, question it, but do it with patience and kind words. Help cast members want to get it right for you.
- Use the system in conjunction with FP+. Disney designed it to work this way, and it does help.

Using Strollers as Wheelchairs

Stroller parking is a big thing at Walt Disney World. Strollers are not allowed in most restaurants or in any attractions. If you use a stroller as a wheelchair, no worries! There is an accessibility card for the stroller that allows you to bring it into areas that typically don't allow them.

- Go to guest services and ask for a pass allowing your stroller to be used as your wheelchair. There is a card that attaches to the stroller so there are no questions at the queues.
- For safety, you must fold the stroller up (even with the wheelchair tag) when on a bus, the Magic Kingdom train, or tram.

Wheel Chair Accessibility

All of the resort is ADA compliant, and there are special entrances to certain areas of the parks that accommodate wheelchairs. If you typically do not use a wheelchair, but you are concerned about all of the extra walking involved, you need to do some research to decide if an Electric scooter (ECV) or a rented wheelchair is more appropriate for your needs.

- Special parking for disabled guests is available. Ask for directions when you enter the main gate.
- If you are driving to the Magic Kingdom, the TTC (Ticket and Transportation Center) has marked parking and the monorail and ferryboats are both accessible, the ferry is easier because there are no steep ramps.
- Theme park disability parking is not close to the park. If you need help, look for a parking attendant to loan you a wheelchair. After you enter the park, you may rent one.
- Most queues are wide enough to accommodate a wheelchair. Very few require a separate entrance.
- If you need an accessible entrance to an attraction, you will be given a paper return pass. Attractions such as Big Thunder Mountain Railroad has a queue with stairs. They bring you and up to 5 guests in through a back way. You will not need a DAS for this accommodation.

- Although most queues are compatible for wheelchairs, ECVs often won't fit. You will be asked to park your ECV and enter the line using a wheelchair they have at the ride.
- There are designated areas to view parades at every theme park and to view the Epcot fireworks. These areas are marked on the park map.
- The monorail ramps are very steep. As long as nobody is very disappointed, the ferry is the best option for getting from the TTC to the Magic Kingdom if you are using a wheelchair.

Wheel Chair Rentals

Walt Disney World does have wheelchairs and ECVs available for rent. They are fine for guests that usually can get around but an injury, walking, or even blisters got the best of them. These conveyances are used a lot and the quality varies. If you know you will need a wheelchair, electric cart, or special stroller, use a rental company. As you will read below, there are many rules and inconveniences with WDW rentals.

- If you are staying at a WDW resort, each has a limited number of complimentary wheelchairs—with a $315 deposit. These chairs are allowed to go all over the resort, including the theme parks.
- If you need to rent a wheelchair at a park, they are available on a first-come, first-served basis for $12 a day; a pre-purchased multi-day pass costs $10 a day. At Disney Springs and the water parks, there is a $100 deposit, and the multi-day pass does not apply. The quality of the chairs varies, and there is never a guarantee that one will be available, even with a multi-day rental.
- There are a limited number of electric carts available for $50 a day with a $20 refundable deposit. A photo ID is required. There is a weight limit of 450 pounds.
- No equipment that is rented in a park may leave that park. If you are headed to another park, return your wheelchair or ECV, make sure you get your receipt, and pick up your refunded deposit. Then you will not have to pay again, you will just need to give the deposit to the new park and show your receipt. Just because the payment transfers, however, does not guarantee an ECV or wheelchair will be available. Be sure you have equipment to help you to get around the rest of the resort. This is another reason to use an outside vendor.
- To ensure availability and flexibility of use, making a reservation with an outside vendor is advisable. They deliver them to your resort and often have added comforts. Choosing a Disney-approved company allows more convenience for pick up and delivery.

Bathrooms

Bathrooms are an important element to a comfortable and successful vacation. Disney has all of the traditional ADA-compliant bathrooms, including the companion bathrooms, throughout the parks and Disney Springs. If you require an adult-sized changing table, the first aid centers have everything you will need, including privacy. Just let the nurse know you need a place to change as you sign in.

First Aid Centers at Magic Kingdom and Hollywood Studios are at the front of the park; Epcot's is at the bridge going into World Showcase (called the Odyssey Building), and Animal Kingdom's is just past Creature Comforts (the Starbucks).

Service Animals

Service animals play an important role in the health, safety, and independence of family members who need them. You might be surprised to learn that the animals are even welcome on many attractions.

Any attraction that is unable to accommodate service animals due to safety reasons has a couple of options. Rider switch can be used with other members of your party. This will allow a family member to wait with the animal while you ride, and then they are able to board the attraction with minimal waiting time so they can join the group soon. You may also bring a portable crate for the animal.

Due to the new pet friendly policy at four of the resorts on Disney property, expect to show the service animals license, just a harness will not work in most cases. Emotional support and therapy animals do not qualify as service animals.

Magic Kingdom

Attractions where service animals are not permitted:

- Space Mountain
- The Barnstormer
- Peter Pan's Flight
- Big Thunder Mountain Railroad
- Splash Mountain

Attractions where service animals are permitted, but use caution:

- Stitch's Great Escape
- Prince Charming Carrousel

Areas for animal relief:

- Tomorrowland, near the Space Mountain restrooms
- Fantasyland, behind the Barnstormer
- Liberty Square, near Princess Tiana
- Frontierland, across from Big Thunder where the sidewalk ends.
- Adventureland, near the Pirate of the Caribbean restrooms

Epcot

Attractions where service animals are not permitted:

- Mission: SPACE
- Test Track
- Soarin'
- Sum of All Thrills (some of the attractions)

Attractions where service animals are permitted, but use caution:

- Spaceship Earth
- Innoventions (certain attractions, such as build a roller coaster)

Areas for animal relief:

- Future World East, next to restrooms behind Mouse Gear
- Future World East, next to the Journey into Imagination restrooms
- United Kingdom pavilion in the World Showcase, to the right of the restrooms
- Norway pavilion in the World Showcase, to the left across from the restrooms

Disney's Hollywood Studios

Attractions where service animals are not permitted:

- Rock 'n' Roller Coaster
- Twilight Zone Tower of Terror
- Star Tours

Attractions where service animals are permitted, but use caution:

- Toy Story Mania

Areas for animal relief:

- In the courtyard near First Aid
- Near Sci-Fi Dine-In Theater

Disney's Animal Kingdom

Attractions where service animals are not permitted:

- In the courtyard near First Aid
- Near Sci-Fi Dine-In Theater
- Expedition Everest
- Primeval Whirl
- DINOSAUR

Attractions where service animals are permitted, but use caution:

- It's Tough to Be a Bug!
- Kilimanjaro Safaris
- Gorilla Falls Exploration Trail (the aviary section)
- Maharajah Jungle Trek (the aviary section)

Areas for animal relief:

- Discovery Island: Near First Aid
- DinoLand USA: Planter next to Restrauntasaurus restrooms
- Asia: Planter to right of Maharajah Jungle Trek restrooms
- Rafiki's Planet Watch: Planter to right of Conservation Station
- Pandora: On path near Satu'li Canteen

As you can imagine, seeing dogs or animals on rides can cause great excitement for many Disney guests (young and old). Be prepared for people wanting to pet your animal and asking for photos. With the crowds, it can be challenging to protect your service animal at times.

Visual Impairments

- Handheld devices are available (for a $25 refundable deposit) that verbally describes each park and many of the attractions.
- Braille guides, menus, and maps are also available.
- Service animals are welcome in the parks.

Hearing Impairments

- Pay phones with TTY (text typewriters) are available throughout Walt Disney World.
- Sign language is available for many shows. Call at least 2 weeks ahead to make arrangements: 407- 824-4321 or 407 827-5141.
- Assistive listening devices for attractions are available for a refundable

$25 deposit at City Hall in Magic Kingdom and at Guest Relations in Epcot, Hollywood Studios, and Animal Kingdom.

- Captioning systems (both reflective and hand held devices) are also available for $25 refundable deposit.

Medication

- All resorts at WDW now offer at least a mini refrigerator in the rooms.
- The first-aid stations in each park offer refrigeration for medicine, and they also have a certified nurse available at all times.
- You may take soft-sided coolers into the park. You may keep them with you or store them in a locker.
- Travel with all of your original bottles and prescriptions. There is a pharmacy that will deliver to the parks, if necessary; simply ask in city hall, guest relations, first aid, or at your resort.

Dietary Restrictions

Food allergies can make eating out stressful, but you can go to any restaurant in WDW and have a choice. Gluten-free is now the most requested dietary need at WDW. When I was discussing the dietary policies with a cast member, she told me about a little boy who said his favorite thing about their vacation was being able to eat in any restaurant he wanted. Usually, that family is limited because of his gluten-free diet, but since Disney has dietary choices at all of its restaurants, he could eat anywhere.

Many people don't understand how important these things are, but knowing there are safe menu items at every place you want to eat (or it will be brought in) makes all the difference in the world to families that struggle with food allergies or special diets.

- If you have any type of dietary restriction, call the dining line at 407939-3463 and discuss your needs with them.
- If you have a general dietary need, ask the host at the front of the restaurant and they will let you know your options. They can even have things from other dining areas brought in to suit your needs.
- When you are making reservations for a table service or character meal, be sure to discuss your needs.

Character Meet and Greets

One of the most significant aspects of raising a child with special needs are emotions. The expectations of meeting Mickey and Minnie are very relevant and can be hard to manage. While preparing for my children's first visit to WDW, I was nervous about how to get that great photo of my kids with Mickey. I was not sure my son, Ben, would go for it, and Meg was only a year old. Still, it was important to me. We did get a great photo, and the kids had fun with the characters. Here are some thing we learned:

- *Relax.* Somehow in the craziness of getting the trip lined up, I focused less on meeting Mickey, and I think that helped.
- *Get autographs.* Collecting autographs gives children a mission. After Ben realized that characters would sign his book, he wanted to see how many autographs he could collect. If they are focusing on getting that book filled, they have less time to get anxious about who they are about to meet. You can purchase autograph books anywhere at WDW, or you can make one at home as a project to get everyone excited about the trip. Remember to pack a fat pen that will fit in Mickey's hand.
- *Remember PhotoPass.* If it takes both parents holding hands as you carefully approach Mickey, who will take the photo? PhotoPass is always ready to capture the shot (but never upset if you don't need them). Also, cast members will use your camera to take photos. Never feel awkward about asking.
- *Come prepared.* Mickey in person doesn't look quite the same as he does on TV. There are live-action Disneyland sing-a-long DVDs, like one called *Disneyland Fun*, that will give your kids a better idea of what to expect. (Check YouTube as well.)
- *Be optimistic.* Children often rise to meet our expectations. If you go to visit Mickey without hesitation, it may be easier than you thought. That was my experience with Ben.
- *Remember recovery time.* Most kids with ASD take longer to recover from upsetting situations than a typical child. If your child does seem frightened, maybe this is not meant to be part of your experience. But remember, it's like sitting on Santa's lap; many kids don't care to do it. It is not necessarily because of ASD, and it shouldn't keep you from having a wonderful vacation.
- *Consider some character dinners.* The easiest way to spend some time with the characters is at a meal. Each character comes to every table and signs autographs, poses for pictures, and interact. The pressure is off while you eat, and it can happen naturally. Also, if it isn't going well, simply let the characters know to move along, and they will.

Amy's Analysis. With a little bit of extra planning, any need you have can be accommodated at Walt Disney World. Do everything you can to plan and prepare, then trust in the system and have a wonderful time.

SECTION TWO

We're Here! Now What?

Taming Disney's Transportation, Dining, and Theme Parks

CHAPTER NINE

WDW Transportation

You're in Orlando! The fun is about to begin.

Magical Express. This is a complimentary shuttle to get to your Disney resort from Orlando International Airport (MCO). It can save you around $160 in taxi or shuttle fees.

- When you decide you want to use the Magical Express, call (407) 939-5277 and give them your flight information.
- You will receive bright yellow luggage tags in the mail. These tags identify your luggage so it can be delivered right to your room. You get to skip baggage claim.
- If your plane will arrive after 10:00pm EST, you will need to go to baggage claim. If you don't want to wait for your bags, go there anyway (the "magic" service can take a couple of hours)
- If you have what you need in your carry-on luggage, follow the signs to baggage claim until you start seeing signs for Magical Express.
- It's fine to take time to stop at the fun shops or grab a bite to eat; you won't lose your ride if you are taking your time.
- Have at least one MagicBand ready and look for a cast member wearing a Mickey hand. They will direct you to the line for your bus.
- The buses are plush, with cartoons and a promotional videos playing.
- They do wait a bit to get a full bus before leaving sometimes.
- Each bus stops at a couple of resorts that are close together.
- Tipping the driver $1 a bag if you chose to bring your luggage, or else a few dollars, is customary.
- The night before you are leaving the resort, a notice from Magical Express will arrive in your room with your departure times.

Transportation and Ticket Center (TTC). As the name implies, the TTC is a hub for different transportation. It begins as the parking lot for the Magic Kingdom and is also the transfer location for the monorail. If you are a guest in a Disney resort, there are no parking fees. If you choose to drive to the parks, simply have them scan your MagicBand or show them your parking pass and park where you like.

- Signs that point you to the Magic Kingdom are actually taking you to the TTC.
- There is handicapped parking at the TTC.
- Some of the parking is far enough away that a tram collects guests and brings them to the front.
- Even with handicapped credentials, you cannot pull up to the Magic Kingdom and drop off a guest. Every car and non-Disney bus goes to the TTC.
- Once at the TTC you may choose a monorail or ferry to get to the Magic Kingdom. The monorail requires a long, steep ramp; the ferry is a flat walk.
- You may also take a monorail to one of the three Magic Kingdom resorts (Contemporary, Polynesian, Grand Floridian) or to Epcot. If you are starting your day at Epcot and ending it at the Magic Kingdom, this is where you want to be parked.

Disney Buses. Most guests in a Disney resort use the buses at least once. If you don't have a car with you, I expect you'll use the buses a lot.

- Buses go almost everywhere, including water parks and Disney Springs, from most resorts (there is no bus to the Magic Kingdom from a resort with a monorail).
- The rule of thumb is buses come every 20 minutes, but that varies quite a bit depending on the time of day.
- There are monitors at the resort bus stops that let you know when the next bus is coming. There are not monitors at the parks or Disney Springs telling you when your next bus will come.
- Buses accommodate ECVs and wheelchairs.
- ECVs and wheelchairs enter the bus first; look for the symbol to the right of the stop. That is where you will board. The bus lowers, the driver comes out and drops a ramp. Because so many EVC drivers are new at this, the drivers often ask to load for you. You and your family board after the EVC is loaded.
- For safety reasons, all strollers must be folded up, even if you have a stroller as wheelchair tag.

Monorail. The most iconic mode of transportation at WDW is the monorail. We love it, but it doesn't go as many places as a lot of people anticipate.

- The monorail goes from the TTC to either Epcot or Magic Kingdom. It also circles the loop of the Magic Kingdom that includes the Contemporary, Grand Floridian, and Polynesian resorts.
- If you are staying in resort that isn't on the monorail and you don't use your car, it is possible to not ride the monorail at all; however, it is always free and I recommend that you at least take a loop around the resorts after a visit to the Magic Kingdom.
- You do not need to fold a stroller on the monorail.
- If you are going from a "monorail resort" or the Magic Kingdom to Epcot, you will need to transfer to a different monorail at the TTC. Watch which ramp you enter, or you could find yourself getting on the wrong monorail.

Ferry. The ferry travels back and forth between the TTC and the Magic Kingdom. It holds a large number of guests, and is completely accessible.

Friendship Boats. These are the boats that travel from a resort to a park. They are a lovely way to avoid big crowds and be on the water.

Minnie Vans. There is a new (as of summer 2017) "Uber-type" service in Disney transportation. A red van with white dots comes and picks you up and will take you anywhere on property. There is a fee of $20 a ride (for the whole family, not per person), and there is no tipping. Car seats and wheelchair lifts or ramps are available, and the drivers are Disney cast members. To use this service go to the front desk of your resort.

Note: The service uses an app serviced by Lyft. You must have a smart phone and be comfortable using your credit card on it to use this service.

Disney Skyliner. The skyliner is an air gondola system that will transport guests to Epcot and Hollywood Studios from the Caribbean Beach, Art of Animation, Pop Century resorts, and the coming-soon Riveira Resort. It was announced in July 2017 with few details. Construction has already begun, but Disney has not announced an opening date or other details.

CHAPTER TEN

The Heart of It All

The four theme parks are where the magic really happens. Here are some of the things that are the same for each park:

Stroller Rental. I suggest you bring your own stroller, but if you aren't able to travel with a stroller, then rent one from a Disney-approved vendor (a list is here: disneyworld.disney.go.com/guest-services/stroller-rentals). If you find yourself in a situation where blisters or tired little legs take you by surprise, there are strollers for rent in each park and at Disney Springs.

- If you pre-pay for the number of days you are going to be in the parks, you can save a few bucks each day with a multi-day pass. Save your receipt and show it each time you need a stroller.
- The strollers can't leave the park. If you are park hopping, you need to return the first stroller, then get a new one when you arrive at the next park. Single-day or multi-day pass holders only need to show their receipt to get another stroller.
- A single stroller is $15 ($13 for multi day).
- A double stroller is $31 ($27 for multi day).

Lockers. Key-operated lockers are available at the front of each park. They can be accessed throughout the day, only. Each day brings with it a new fee and locker, so do not leave items overnight.

- Small (11"x9"x16") costs $8 per day, with a $5 key deposit.
- Large (17.5"x 12"x16") costs $10 a day, with a $5 key deposit.

Food. You are welcome to bring food and unopened drinks into the parks. Small soft-sided coolers are permitted.

First Aid. The first aid stations in the parks are prepared for anything. They can store medicine and diabetes supplies, and help with any medical support you need. Look on the resort maps for locations.

Childcare Centers. The childcare centers are a wonderful spot to take care of some important needs. If you need diapers and supplies or lost your last pacifier, you can find what you need here. Some items are complimentary, others are for sale. There are large changing rooms where you can tend to adults with diaper needs. It is a calm, air-conditioned space with a TV and high chairs, plus nursing areas.

Rider Switch. On select attractions, if a guest doesn't meet the height requirement, or a guest that doesn't want to ride the attraction, both parents can still enjoy it without waiting in line twice. Here's how it works:

- Check in with the cast member at the front of the ride to make sure it qualifies.
- The entire party needs to check in together with the cast member "greeting" at that attraction.
- At least one adult must stay with the guest not riding the attraction. The cast member will give that adult the rider switch pass and asked them to wait outside the attraction.
- The group not riding the attraction first can go have fun somewhere else.
- After the first group finishes, the group that hasn't ridden has 5 days to ride it. So, you can either go right away, or wait.
- When the second group arrives at the ride, they will present the pass and go to the FastPass line.
- You can use this on attractions for which you also have FastPasses.
- Any attraction with a height requirement has ride switch.

CHAPTER ELEVEN

The Magic Kingdom

The Magic Kingdom is everything the name implies. Since 1971 it has been creating magical vacations. It is the park that you imagine when thinking of Disney World, with its beautiful architecture, spectacular entertainment, and unparalleled commitment to detail and service. Somehow the Magic Kingdom also balances being modern while keeping the innocence and beauty that is signature Disney.

Park Layout

There are 6 themed "lands" in the Magic Kingdom; they are laid out in an arrangement that resembles a wagon wheel. There are shortcuts and pathways to cut in between if you like, but basically it's a big circle.

The entrance for the park takes you under a classic train station into Main Street, U.S.A. Just as the name implies, it is a beautiful town complete with a town hall, fire station, and the a grand emporium. There are also beautiful candy shops and a bakery with Starbucks as you travel up Main Street. At the end of Main Street is Cinderella Castle and a large round gathering space called the hub. If you look to your left you will see the entrance to Adventureland. The other lands follow in this order:

- Frontierland
- Liberty Square
- Fantasyland
- Tomorrowland
- Main Street, U.S.A.

If you go straight through the castle you will see Prince Charming's Regal Carrousel, and that of course, is Fantasyland.

City Hall. This is the guest relations for the park. The cast members here can answer any questions you may have. If someone in your party requires a (DAS), make sure this is your first stop. It is located on your left after you pass under the train station.

Baby Care Center. The center is located at the castle end of Main Street to the left, between Casey's Corner and the Crystal Palace.

First Aid. First Aid is located next to the Child Care Center at the castle end of Main Street, between Casey's Corner and the Crystal Palace. In addition to medical concerns, the First Aid accommodates adult changing needs.

ATMs. There are four ATMs in the Magic Kingdom: near the locker rentals, inside City Hall, inside the exit for Space Mountain, and near Pinocchio's Village Haus restaurant in Fantasyland.

FastPass+ Kiosks. FastPass plus allows you to select 3 FastPasses before you arrive at WDW using the MyDisneyExperience web site or app. Kiosks to make new or extra FastPasses are located in these areas:

- Adventureland, near the Jungle Cruise
- Frontierland, near the Diamond Horseshoe Revue
- Liberty Square, near Hall of Presidents
- Fantasyland, near Mickey's PhilharMagic
- Tomorrowland, near Stitch's Great Escape

Sensory Spots. These areas are good for taking a break and calming down. Some are quieter and out of the way, others are places perfect for running. You'll find them:

- Near the restrooms in Adventureland across from the Swiss Family Treehouse there is an area with 3 half-circle benches. They are covered and receive air conditioning from the adjoining store. Other family members can get Dole Whip or explore the treehouse while you rest.
- Tom Sawyer Island.
- Casey Jr. Splash and Soak. This one is wet, but fun with no time constraints. Behind Casey Jr. there is a tent near a snack cart that is cool, quiet, and out of the way.
- Between Fantasyland and Tomorrowland (behind Dumbo) there is a walkway with room to run back and forth. Unfortunately, the benches are the smoking area, but you can stay as long as you like.
- The Tomorrowland Transit Authority People Mover.

DAS Card vs FastPass+

Trying to plan an itinerary for a family needing assistance has a couple of challenges. Everything is very personal depending on how adventurous your family is, how much you will choose to split up, etc. The lists below are designed to help you make decisions about which FastPass+ choices to make for the Magic Kingdom, compared to getting a DAS reservation.

A suggested rule of thumb is to use FastPass+ for the attractions with the longest wait times. DAS is based on posted wait times, so the shorter those times are, the more you should be able to get in. Here are my recommendation for getting a DAS or FP+:

DAS

- Town Square Theater
- The Magic Carpets of Aladdin
- Jungle Cruise
- Pirates of the Caribbean
- "it's a small world"
- Mickey's PhilharMagic
- The Many Adventures of Winnie the Pooh
- Mad Tea Party
- Under the Sea~Journey of The Little Mermaid
- Ariel's Grotto
- Dumbo the Flying Elephant
- The Barnstormer
- Buzz Lightyear's Space Ranger Spin

FP+

- Splash Mountain
- Big Thunder Mountain
- Haunted Mansion
- Peter Pan's Flight
- Enchanted Tales with Belle
- Seven Dwarfs Mine Train
- Tomorrowland Speedway
- Space Mountain
- Parades

Note we suggested more than 3 FP+. Not everyone chooses to visit all of those attractions. Also, many rides like Haunted Mansion and Space Mountain will not interest the member of your family that requires a DAS, but other family members might choose to ride them. In this case, you need the FastPasses because a DAS can only be used with the guest needing assistance.

Also, a DAS isn't available for the "3:00 Parade." However, if you have a physical disability, there are reserved sections for viewing.

Main Street, U.S.A.

Main Street, U.S.A. is a model of America when Walt Disney was young. Inspired by his childhood home of Marceline, Missouri, it is an excellent backdrop that allows you to leave everything in the real world behind and prepare yourself for a day of magical adventures.

The Walt Disney World Railroad

Ride
Standard wheelchair / Handheld Captioning

The Walt Disney World Railroad includes four antique steam engine trains that take you on a relaxing 20-minute ride around the perimeter of the park. The ride has three station stops: Main Street, Frontierland, and Fantasyland. You may choose to stay on the train or depart any time you'd like. Tell the kids Walt Disney enjoyed trains so much he had one he could ride with his children in his own backyard!

Sensory Impact. This is a great ride for the times you need to slow things down a little. It is also a nice way to get to the exit at the end of the day.

Main Street Vehicles

Ride
Must Transfer

There are period cars, horse-drawn carriages, and a double-decker bus that travel up and down Main Street, and you are welcome to grab a ride. Typically, the last ride can be as early as 10:30 am. There are stops in Town Square and at Cinderella Castle. Riding down Main Street in style feels grand, and what a great photo. The rides are one way. If a member of your party is staying behind with a large stroller or wheelchair, have them meet you at the other end (foldable strollers are fine).

Sensory Impact. No worries.

Sorcerers of the Kingdom

Interactive Game
Accessible

Sorcerers of the Kingdom is an interactive role-playing game that takes you through Main Street, U.S.A., Adventureland, Fantasyland, and Liberty Square. Hades (the villain in the movie *Hercules*) wants to make the Magic Kingdom his home. There are special portals throughout the Magic Kingdom that Merlin and his apprentice sorcerers (that's you) are protecting to make sure Hades can't reassemble the Crystal of the Magic Kingdom and have his way. Each portal (screen) has different Disney characters to cheer you on and congratulate you on conquering the villain.

To become an apprentice sorcerer, simply go to the firehouse on Main Street or behind the Olde Christmas Shoppe in Liberty Square and ask for a starter deck of cards and your key. The cast member will give you cards and a map. They will also explain everything you need to know. It is a cool "adventure" that allows you to interact as a family, and possibly go to areas of the park you haven't visited before.

When we allow Ben to play we emphasize that there will only be one quest per trip, and we remind him we must take breaks to do other things (like eat or ride rides). Many of you reading this book do not have a child that can follow those rules, and it isn't always easy for us, either. So if it looks like it could derail your day, avoid it.

We have been pleasantly surprised to see Ben's social skills shine while playing the game. The cards are tradeable, and he has made trades with other kids. He has also helped other kids understand what to do. If your child needs to work on problem solving or map skills, this is an excellent way to do that. Very often Meg and I go do girl stuff during quest time and meet up with the boys for meals and the occasional FastPass+ or DAS ride reservation. This summer Ben almost missed a FastPass+ to see Elsa. That is how powerful the pull of this game can be.

Also, the cards and map are a cool, free souvenir. You can keep the cards, bring them to your next vacation, and grow your collection.

Sorcerers of the Kingdom is a great experience that can take a lot of time. It is better suited for annual passholders or families taking a longer vacation.

Sensory Impact. The game does involve villains; it can be intense and sometimes startling. However, you are in the bright park and watching a small screen, so the impact is minimal.

Parades

Live Show
Accessible (look for the roped off sections)

The streets are filled with fun music, huge floats, and so many characters you can't help but smile and even dance along. This is a great way to see many Mickey and many of his friends in a non-threatening environment. Check the times guide they give you when you enter the park for current parade information and times, and get there at least 20 minutes early to ensure a good viewing spot.

There are two different parades each day:

- Move It! Shake It! Dance & Play It! Street Party (a shorter parade on Main Street)
- Disney Festival of Fantasy Parade (a bigger parade with a much longer route

Sensory Impact. Loud. I would suggest headphones. There can also be a lot of standing in one place for long periods of time.

Town Square Theater

Character Meet and Greet
Accessible (ramp is to your right)

In this attraction, Mickey talks. His mouth moves, his eyes blink, and he has pre-recorded scripts ready to share with your family. If you're concerned that this might be "creepy," we had that thought, too, but we were wrong. It creates a truly personal experience with your family. There is a lot of Disney magic at play, but it feels authentic, especially to the children. Tinker Bell, of course, always talks to you (as do all of the princesses, wherever you meet them). You may use your own camera or avail yourself of PhotoPass.

This is a whole new way to meet Mickey. Deciding if it is appropriate for your family is a personal choice. If you do decide to attend, you may want to come up with an excuse if any questions arise.

Note that it requires separate FastPasses to see Mickey and Tinker Bell.

A word about the character visits. Many people think being comfortable meeting with Mickey and friends is one of the criteria for being a good candidate to visit Disney World. There is so much more to a happy vacation than a successful visit with Mickey Mouse. Many neuro-typical children don't like seeing Mickey, and everyone still has a fabulous vacation.

Sensory Impact. Explaining that Mickey talks to you at the theater, but not when you meet him at Chef Mickey's, can be a challenge. Also, Minnie, Goofy, and the other "masked" characters don't talk when you meet them. The other sensory concern is if you have a family member that will really want answers from Mickey. His phrases are very general and follow a pre-scripted experience. If you suspect your family member will get frustrated when not getting the right response, you may want to meet Mickey in another location, either at a different park or during a character meal.

Happily Ever After

Fireworks and Light Projection Show
Accessible (look for the roped off sections)

A truly iconic ending to a day at Magic Kingdom is fireworks exploding in all of their beauty over Cinderella Castle. When I was a kid it was amazing to have a soundtrack that was synchronized with the fireworks. Now artists use the technology to not only sync music, but an entire show projected on the castle featuring classic and modern Disney favorites. All of this, plus Tinker Bell flying over your head. It really is an amazing show.

However, it is also the most challenging show for a guest with special needs. In order to fully experience the show you must be facing the front of Cinderella's Castle. Unfortunately, thousands of other guests all want to do this, too. Getting a good spot requires waiting for at least 30 minutes, if not more. Obviously, being near rest rooms, getting anxious in crowds, and not being able to be still are all challenges for this situation. I have two suggestions for easier viewing. You can go to the train station and watch it from the boarding platform. There aren't as many people and it is more contained (it also helps you leave easier). If there is room in your budget you can go to a dessert party, which includes a VIP viewing area and plenty of room. I suggest the plaza garden view; it is less expensive and a better view. You can make reservations through Disney dining.

Sensory Impact: High alert, but the experience is so special that with some planning and headphones it might be worth it.

Adventureland

Come fly on a magic carpet, become a pirate, and be transported into a faraway land of adventure. Be aware, you never know when a pirate is sneaking up behind you, or a camel is spitting.

Pirates of the Caribbean

Boat Ride
Transfer Twice / Handheld Captioning / Audio Description

Yo Ho, Yo Ho, a pirate's life for me.... Dive into the life of Captain Jack Sparrow and experience the pirate's life for yourself. This boat ride will take you to the dark, and often funny, life of pirates. Watch to see how many times Captain Jack pops up during the ride.

If your little princesses are at the Bibbidi Bobbidi Boutique, the young men in your life may want to become a pirate. The Pirates League is next door to the Pirates of the Caribbean. It offers face painting and pirate lessons.

Sensory Impact. This ride seems like it should be scary, but I have never really seen anyone get upset. It's so mesmerizing that you are transformed and not frightened. Besides, there are funny dogs and pigs to distract you. There are moments of darkness and a light mist, but no loud noises or startling moments. A couple of dips can get you a little wet. If splashes concern you, ask to sit further back in the boat.

Note: There is a new PhotoPass experience, but because the ride is dark, the flash is very bright. In addition, the queue is very loud. Using FastPass or DAS to avoid the noise is recommended.

Jungle Cruise

Boat Ride
Accessible / Assistive Listening / Sensory friendly

Adventure awaits on a boat ride through the jungle, where you will see elephants, tigers, and hippos! Walt Disney insisted on consistency throughout his park. Animals are anything but consistent, so instead of bringing in a real "zoo-type" attraction, he created Audio-Animatronics animals that would always "perform" the same. No sleeping tigers, or elephants pooping; every ride is perfect (though many 10 year olds love to see elephants poop).

The ride can feel a little out dated, especially now that the Animal Kingdom is open, but if someone in your family is an animal lover, then it won't disappoint—and the jokes are first-rate tacky puns.

Sensory Impact. This is an easy boat ride. A few of the jokes could be intimidating if taken literally.

Walt Disney's Enchanted Tiki Room

Audio-Animatronics Musical Show
Accessible / Assistive Listening / Handheld Captioning / Audio Description

Welcome to the Tiki Room where many enchanted birds are ready to entertain you. This is a classic, but the show can be a little scary with a storm scene that can be frightening.

Sensory Impact. There is a lot to be concerned about. It is loud and at times intense, with lots of bird movement, noisy singing, and a "thunderstorm" outside. If a member of your group doesn't do well in loud, semi-dark enclosed spaces, or is afraid of thunderstorms, skip this attraction.

The Magic Carpets of Aladdin

Attraction Type: Ride
Standard Wheelchair Then Transfer

Soar up in the air on a magic carpet just like Aladdin and Princess Jasmine. This "Dumbo-style" ride flies in a circle and the joystick allows you to go up and down. Be sure to look out for the camel...he spits!

Sensory Impact. No worries!

Swiss Family Treehouse

Attraction Type: Walkthrough
Ambulatory / Sensory friendly

The Robinson family was stranded on an island for years. They were quite inventive in creating a functional home with all of the things they rescued from the shipwreck. Walk up and down the steps while looking in all of their "rooms" to see how they lived.

Sensory Impact. This attraction has you walk in a line up the treehouse and down again. There isn't any interaction or chance to fully explore. Anyone who gets impatient easily may want to sit this one out.

Frontierland

Saddle up and come along on for a Hootin' Tootin' good time! Runaway train rides, free falls into briar patches, and exploring an island like good ole Tom Sawyer, what could be more fun?

Big Thunder Mountain Railroad

Thrill Ride (height requirement 40")
Must Transfer / Good Health / No Service Animals

This is not a loop de loop, and it doesn't have any really big hills, but it is an enjoyable fast paced coaster. It is really perfect for people that are just discovering roller coasters, and guests that like their rides to kick it up a notch after a few story-telling rides.

Sensory Impact. The first climb is very loud, headphones are recommended. This is a faster paced ride that does have a tiny bit of scary bones and western type décor.

Splash Mountain

Thrill Ride (height requirement 40")
Must Transfer / Good Health / No Service Animals

"Please don't throw me in that briar patch!" may be one of the best bluffs ever told, but let's see how it feels to actually be thrown into the briar patch... it feels *wet*! This is a wonderful flume ride with a couple of little surprises and one big surprise. It follows the tale of Br'er Rabbit from the movie *Song of the South*, with a heart-stopping 5 story plunge into the briar patch.

Sensory Impact. This is a sweet ride with no noises or things to startle you, but you do get very wet, and it can be a very scary drop at the end. Also, sensitive souls could be quite nervous for "poor" Br'er Rabbit.

Country Bear Jamboree

Audio-Animatronics Show
Accessible / Assistive Listening / Reflective Captioning

Come sit a spell and enjoy a show. This is a classic comedy musical show that I remember being very funny as a child. I'll admit, I don't enjoy this one any longer and neither do my kids. But humor is very personal. If you choose to check it out, it's only 12 minutes long.

Sensory Impact. It's air conditioned and gives everyone a chance to sit down.

Tom Sawyer Island

Sensory Break
Ambulatory

Have an adventure and explore the island just like Tom Sawyer would. First you ride on a raft to get there, then the island is yours to explore. You may stay as long as you like (except it closes at dusk) and run as fast and as hard as you can. This is truly the most underrated attraction in the Magic Kingdom. There are rope bridges to cross, caves to explore, rocks to climb, and a large fort (where there are more restrooms). There used to be a little snack shop where you could get lemonade and snacks, but now I would recommend bringing a snack to the island with you if you plan to stay awhile.

Tom Sawyer Island is the perfect place for a sensory break. If you are not able to get back to your hotel to decompress for a little bit, plan on spending an extra long time here. If it were accessible, it would be perfect.

Sensory Impact. This is not a wheelchair friendly area, and some of the special touches are scary. The cave is larger than it seems, is dark and crowded, and can make you feel lost. Luckily, the cave can be avoided and there are still playgrounds and a lot of places to run.

Liberty Square

Listen for the drum and fife as you enter Liberty Square surrounded by cobblestones and patriotic bunting. Children better mind their manners or their parents may put them in the stocks!

Haunted Mansion

Dark Ride
Must Transfer / Handheld Captioning / Audio Description

Come visit the "Grim Grinning Ghosts" that occupy the Mansion of Liberty Square. Naturally the ghosts are far more funny than scary, and there is NEVER anything violent or gory, but all the same some guests get nervous and really do not see it as the charming ride that it is. If you have a family member that seemed more brave than they turn out to be there is a "chicken door" and all you have to do is ask a cast member yes, we know this from experience.

Sensory Impact. There are no obvious sensory issues, but the content alone can make some more anxious than necessary. Also, at the end of the ride you see in the mirror that you have a visitor in your car with you, this could seem too real for someone that doesn't get the magic of it all. There's a moving sidewalk to enter and exit the ride (assistance will be given if needed).

The Hall of Presidents

Audio-Animatronics Show
Accessible / Assistive Listening / Reflective Captioning

Note: At press time, this attraction is under refurbishment without an opening date scheduled.

Come and see all the presidents of the United States on stage together. They are not simply wax figures; they come to life (some of them more than others). My family are history geeks, so we love it. It may not appeal to everyone.

This attraction showcases the technology that helped propel Walt Disney's movies and theme parks into something magical. It is interesting to see how much some of the presidents truly look like themselves, and it is a cool and restful auditorium.

Sensory Impact. This is a temperature-controlled. quiet, dark place to rest, and maybe learn a thing or two.

Liberty Square Riverboat

Boat Ride
Accessible

If you are looking for an activity to slow down a little, step onto the Mark Twain riverboat and take a leisurely cruise down the Rivers of America.

Sensory Impact. This is a nice, easy-going time, with no worries!

The Muppets Present Great Moments in History

Puppet Show
Outdoors; no seating

The town crier is gathering everyone around the Hall of Presidents to hear the lessons of this fine country as only the Muppets can tell it. Kermit, Miss Piggy, Gonzo, Fozzie, and ever-patriotic, Sam the Eagle use storytelling, song, fun costuming, and Muppet humor to share a piece of America's story. There are two different shows each around 10 minutes long, with multiple showings per day. We like to sit on the planters outside the Hall of Presidents because it is shaded, but a more direct view is across the street. This show doesn't attract a large crowd so there is no reason to arrive extra early. The Liberty Square market is nearby, making it a great time to have a snack and see a show.

Sensory Impact. There is no cover from the weather. If lightning is in the area, the show will abruptly end. Otherwise, there are no worries during the show itself.

Fantasyland

Princesses, fairies, circus trains, the most lovable bear there ever was, and the only place you can see elephants fly.

Dumbo the Flying Elephant

Ride
Must Transfer

Dumbo is one of the most popular rides in the Magic Kingdom. It is so popular that they made an identical ride so guests can get through the lines twice as fast. With the redesign of Fantasyland, Dumbo has been relocated to the new circus area. It's located as you enter Fantasyland coming from the Tomorrowland walkway or from the train station. It is a very simple ride that flies you in a circle while you use a joystick to go up and down.

Sensory Impact. No worries! There is nothing loud, however it does fly, so a fear of heights could be challenging. There is also an indoor play space to help with the wait time.

The Barnstormer

Roller Coaster (height Restriction 35")
Must Transfer / Expectant Mothers Should Not Ride / No Service Animals

Come with the Great Goofini to soar into the sky on a perfect introduction to roller coasters. This is a very quick ride with a mild up-and-down track. Barnstormer may look familiar: it was originally in Toon Town when Goofy was a crop duster. It has been restyled to fit with the new circus area of Fantasyland.

Sensory Impact. This is a mild ride with a roller-coaster feel. There are a couple of "hills" that shouldn't frighten children, though there are always exceptions. An easy coaster, especially since there is little noise or effects.

Casey Jr. Splash and Soak Station

Water Play Area
Accessible

Casey Jr. is right on schedule to help you cool down and run off some steam. This adorable circus train is designed to splash kids, and adults, who would like to get wet. There are no time limits, and there are plenty of areas on low brick walls for you to sit and watch the kids play.

Kids that enjoy being sprayed will get soaked. You may want to come prepared with a change of clothes and some swim shoes. The idea is to cool off, so a towel wouldn't be a priority for me, but dry feet might be. There is a kiosk that has for sale swim diapers, sunscreen, towels, swim suits, and anything else you might need.

Sensory Impact. A great place for a sensory break, with plenty of water. If the weather is hot, it's a great mood lifter for tired and hot kids, or for those feeling a bit overwhelmed.

Pete's Silly Side Show

Character Meet and Greet
Accessible

Meet some of Mickey's friends under the Big Top. This is where you meet Minnie, Donald, and Goofy at scheduled times.

Sensory Impact. This is a rather quiet section of the park. There is also a hot dog stand and tables under cover that make for a good space to be out of the crowd.

Mad Tea Party

Ride
Must Transfer

Alice and the Mad Hatter would like to invite you to tea. Of course, this isn't like a proper tea party. The teacups keep spinning! This ride is an all-time favorite in my family. We often laugh while remembering when different people rode together and how fast we would spin them. My son is hypo-sensitive, so this attraction is a win-win for us.

Sensory Impact. If you are hypo-sensitive (like to swing forever without getting dizzy), this ride is great to help regulate your vestibular system. If you are not good with spinning, sit this one out.

Enchanted Tales With Belle

Story Telling, Character Meet and Greet
Handheld Captioning / Audio Description / Standard Wheelchair

Visit Maurice's workshop, and magically arrive in Beast's Castle. Help Lumière tell the "Tale As Old As Time." Little guests help re-create the story of Beauty and the Beast, and are greeted by Belle. Many children (and some dads) are chosen to be in the show. If a child really wants to be in the show, but wasn't chosen, no worries—there are plenty of enchanted objects available to give everyone a chance to participate. And if you do not wish to participate, that is completely fine, too.

At the beginning, when you are in the workshop, stay to the back. The crowd pushes forward. It won't matter where you are in just a couple of minutes.

Sensory Impact. No worries.

Under the Sea~Journey of the Little Mermaid

Ride

Standard Wheelchair / Handheld Captioning / Audio Description

Scuttle is your guide on a clamshell ride through Ariel's story of how she became a human married to Prince Eric. This ride is all about the fabulous soundtrack.

Sensory Impact. Minimal; many will not need the headphones. Ursula is of course large, and fairly close to your clam shell, but you keep moving, making it not too intense. There's a moving sidewalk to enter and exit the ride (assistance will be given if needed).

Ariel's Grotto

Character Meet and Greet

Accessible

Meet Ariel as she was in her mermaid days. Parents, feel free to use your own camera in addition to PhotoPass.

Sensory Impact. Any Ariel fan that chooses to meet her will be fine.

The Many Adventures of Winnie the Pooh

Ride

Handheld Captioning / Audio Description / Standard Wheelchair

Climb into a honey pot and travel through the story of *Winnie the Pooh and the Blustery Day.* Your honey pot bounces with Tigger, rolls with the wind, and even spends some time in the dark with Heffalumps and Woozles. For a reason I still have not figured out, I have seen several children exit the ride screaming. My daughter, who is typically developing, was terrified as a one year old. We even tried it again because we thought maybe she had been tired (and she loved Pooh); but more screaming. So for a ride that seems mild, it can have unexpected effects on some children.

Sensory Impact. This ride is a familiar story to most kids that are visiting WDW. That can help with all of the stimulation in the ride. Headphones would be helpful if they are comforting for a person with ASD. There are a couple of short periods of darkness, a simulated storm, and the dream sequence does have Heffalumps and Woozles.

Pooh's Thotful Spot

Character Meet and Greet

Accessible

Next to the Winnie the Pooh ride you can meet Pooh and Tigger. Consider dining at the Crystal Palace if you would like to meet Eeyore and Piglet, too.

Sensory Impact. No worries!

Seven Dwarfs Mine Train

Roller Coaster (height requirement 38")
Must Transfer / Expectant Mothers Should Not Ride / No Service Animals

Swinging mine cars travel through the Seven Dwarfs mine and lead them home. This is a "mini mountain," a world-class ride on a smaller scale. Beautifully designed, with some fun hills, turns, and speed, yet not as intense as the other WDW "mountains." This attraction is a great bridge to the "big-time" rides.

Sensory Impact. There is singing (but not terribly loud), and no instances of complete darkness. The track can seem loud to some, but it is not as loud as other rides in the park. If you are seated toward the front of the train, at the very end of the ride you could be next to the witch for a short time. If this is an issue, board the car first and you might not even see her.

Princess Fairytale Hall

Character Meet and Greet
Accessible

Come and meet some princesses, get autographs, and photos. The princesses will spend a couple of minutes getting to know you.

In each line you get to meet two princesses. For example, one line might have both Rapunzel and Princess Tiana. Then a different line might have Snow White and Princess Aurora (Sleeping Beauty). Each line has its own FastPass; however, I would use your FastPasses on other attractions.

The princesses available sometimes change, but only princesses that don't have a permanent home (like Ariel's Grotto) will be here.

Sensory Impact. No worries!

"it's a small world"

Boat Ride
Standard Wheelchair / Handheld Captioning / Audio Description

With a song that is so catchy it may never leave your head, "it's a small world" has been a symbol for Disney since the ride was first developed for the 1964 New York Worlds Fair. After the fair, the ride was relocated to Disneyland in California. Many people enjoy making fun of the ride, but children really enjoy seeing the places they are just starting to learn about represented in colorful dolls, while singing a song about peace (over and over again). My Ben and I love it!

Sensory Impact. No worries!

Peter Pan's Flight

Dark Ride

Ambulatory / Handheld Captioning / Audio Description / No Service Animals

Fly away in a pirate's ship to Neverland through the story of Peter Pan. Your ride vehicle "flies" above the scenes as you look down on the story of Captain Hook, Peter Pan, Mary, and Tinker Bell. This is a popular ride that uses Audio Animatronics, black light, and pixie dust to bring this classic story to life.

Sensory Impact. It is dark, and it flies (you look down on the ride), so a fear of heights could be an issue. There's a moving sidewalk to enter and exit the ride (assistance will be given if needed).

Mickey's PhilharMagic

4D Movie

Accessible / Assistive Listening / Reflective Captioning / Audio Description

Imagine what would happen if Donald Duck borrowed the sorcerer's hat. That is just what happens in this crazy musical journey through some of Disney's most beloved movies. Remember to keep in mind Donald's temper...it can disturb some.

A 4D movie means it is 3D with some extras like bubbles floating down, scents, and little sprits of water, but nothing scary.

As the cast members are directing you into the theater, stay to the back. They really pack the hall while you are waiting for the interior doors to open. It can be too crowded for people with crowd issues to feel comfortable. There really isn't a seat that's too far back.

Sensory Impact. If you have been to a 3D movie, you have a pretty good idea what to expect. It can be loud. Headphones are a must.

Prince Charming's Regal Carrousel

Old-Fashioned Carousel

Must Transfer / Service Animals Permitted with Caution

Enjoy this majestic carousel with beautiful murals from *Cinderella* and music from a classic calliope. Choose a horse to ride or sit in a carriage or sleigh as you survey the kingdom.

Sensory Impact. No worries, as long as they hold on tight and don't mind going in circles.

Cinderella Castle

Walkthrough

Accessible

Beautifully reaching up into the sky, Cinderella Castle represents all of the fairytales. As you walk through it, you will see large murals, made of glass like her slippers, telling the story of Cinderella and how she met her prince. Then, as the story ends, you are in Fantasyland.

Cinderella Castle has a beautiful restaurant on an upper floor and the Bibbidi Bobbidi Boutique toward the Fantasyland end, where fairy godmothers in training do your hair, nails, wardrobe, and of course, sprinkle you with pixie dust so you look like the princess you are as you enjoy the rest of your day in the Magic Kingdom.

Many families believe the castle makes a great "meet me if we get separated and phones die place." I would come up with a better location that is meaningful to your party. There are often large crowds and shows at the castle, making it more challenging to see the people you are looking for.

Tomorrowland

The future is within reach, and the attractions can take you to infinity and beyond in this exciting land. It may not seem as futuristic as it did in 1971, but the décor is still effective at making you feel you are in a world years ahead of your time.

Tomorrowland Speedway

Ride (height requirement 32"; 54" to drive)
Must Transfer / Good Health

Who doesn't dream of being a race car driver? Here is your chance to drive a mini gas-powered racecar around the .4-mile speedway. Rails help to keep you on the right track as you race up to 7 mph. Don't forget to wave to your fans as you pass under the covered observation bridge.

Sensory Impact. The engines are noisy, but with headphones on, this really is a fun, easy ride. The fumes can be overwhelming, and the queue can be quite hot. Be sure to use a FastPass+ or DAS reservation.

Stitch's Great Escape

Multi-Sensory Experience (height Requirement 40")
Standard Wheelchair / Assistive Listening / Hand held Listening / Video Captioning / Service Animals Permitted With Caution

Note: This attraction has become a meet and greet for Stitch when not operating. No dates have been published concerning operation dates.

You are trainee for the Galactic Federation Security Agency minimum-security facility. On your first day a new prisoner is being transferred into the facility and you are asked to help guard Experiment 626, aka Stitch. He is a little more high maintenance than they are used to dealing with, so plan on lots of craziness on this adventure. (The attraction now seasonal, and open only during busy seasons.)

Sensory Impact. This attraction has odd smells, a lot of darkness, suspense, flashing lights, and a theme that may be too intense for young children or anyone with sensory issues. It also pinches your shoulders, and it actually hurts a little (or a lot). I do not recommend it.

Monsters, Inc. Laugh Floor

Interactive Show
Accessible / Assistive Listening / Video Captioning

Monsters Inc. needs you...to laugh! Monstropolis needs laughs for power, and Mike Wazowski and friends have a comedy club so they can entertain you *and* harness your laughter. This is an interactive digital attraction that allows you to text a joke and maybe become part of the show.

Sensory Impact. Minimal, the crowd's reactions are usually moderate laughter, but a rowdy family nearby could be loud. Typically this is a fun space and a nice cool break.

Buzz Lightyear's Space Ranger Spin

Ride
Standard Wheelchair / Handheld captioning / Audio Description

This attraction feels like a life-sized video game. You use your space cruiser to ride through the galaxy while you shooting targets and earning points with your laser cannon (which shoots a thin point of light). The fun memories of this attraction last to infinity and beyond.

Sensory Impact. This attraction is dark with some flashing lights. Points are scored, so if you have a competitive family member that will get very upset, have a plan before riding. There's a moving sidewalk to enter and exit the ride (assistance will be given if needed).

Meet Buzz Lightyear

Character Meet and Greet
Accessible

Buzz Lightyear is stationed next to his attraction. He's ready to meet you, take photos, and stamp your autograph book.

Astro Orbiter

Ride
Must Transfer

Soar high above Tomorrowland and enjoy the spectacular view. Pilot your 2-person rocket to go up and down as you orbit the tower. The entrance of the attraction is at the bottom of the PeopleMover; just look for the elevators. The view makes this basic ride a little more extraordinary.

Sensory Impact. The ride is very high up, so a person that's afraid of heights may have some concerns. There is also a high step to get into the rocket, without handles (think getting into a high car).

Tomorrowland Transit Authority People Mover

Ride

Ambulatory / Handheld Captioning / Audio Description

Enjoy your guided tour of Tomorrowland from a personal cart on the moving sidewalk high above everyone's heads. Zoom through Space Mountain (from a much calmer vantage point), Buzz Lightyear's Space Ranger Spin, and other points of interest in Tomorrowland. This is a perfect way to get a taste of Tomorrowland and decide what your family would like to do.

Sensory Impact. The PeopleMover is a great ride for when you need a quiet moment or a little break. We have been known to ride it several times in a row. There's a moving Sidewalk (and a steep ramp that is a moving sidewalk) to enter and exit ride (assistance will be given if needed).

Walt Disney's Carousel of Progress

Show

Accessible / Assistive Listening / Handheld Captioning / Audio Description

This is an attraction created by Walt Disney and the Disneyland Imagineers for the 1964 World's Fair. It is a journey through the 20th century, to look at how technology improves our way of life. It is not current, but it is Disney history. It's a nice break from the sun, and my family enjoys seeing just how far we've come while discussing the many thing that aren't in the attraction. Plus, Ben loves the jokes.

Sensory Impact. This is a quiet, dark, comfortable "ride" that is a great break.

Space Mountain

Roller Coaster (height requirement 44")

Transfer Twice / No Service Animals

Are you ready to launch into space on a ride you will never forget? Space Mountain is an indoor roller coaster that propels you into space on a very twisty, bumpy, and dark ride. It was the first of the "mountains" in Walt Disney World, and for decades it has been a favorite attraction.

Sensory Impact. This is a big-time ride. It doesn't go upside down, and there are no big hills. However, it is fast, dark, has flashing lights, and is very jerky. I would make sure everyone *really* wants to ride this one! Another consideration: the rocket ships you ride in are not easy to climb in and out of. They are low, and stepping in and out of them takes some maneuvering if you are not a young, skinny kid. And remember, people with

ASD often take a long time to recover. Consider riding these high-impact rides carefully before you do it. It is not worth it to make a person ride something just so you can use a DAS; it could make the rest of your day very challenging.

Park Exit and Analysis

Some tips for exiting the Magic Kingdom:

- If you are near a train station and you are ready to leave the park, hopping a ride on the train can be an easy option. But remember, the trains stop running at dusk(ish).
- If you are using the monorail, be sure to notice which track to use. One of them is for resorts only.

Magic Kingdom. The name says it all. For me, it really is a *Magic* Kingdom. But a few tips do help the park to fulfill its magical potential. Get there as early as your family can manage it. As the day gets later, the park fills up. Having a little room and some shorter wait times helps to start the day off well. Look out for fatigue; if you are proactive with sensory spots or breaks, meltdowns will be at a minimum. Finally, to quote Elsa, "Let it Go!" If there is a hiccup in the plan, just move forward and continue to enjoy yourselves; nobody has everything go right, even with the magic of Disney.

Coming Soon...

Tron Lightcycle Power Run, a roller coaster similar to Shanghai Disneyland's TRON Lightcycle, will be constructed in this area of the park close to Space Mountain. Few details are available at press time.

CHAPTER TWELVE

Epcot

Epcot is an acronym for Experimental Prototype Community of Tomorrow. Walt Disney's original vision was to build a "city of the future" with ideal situations for work, rest, and play. His grand plans included airports, homes, and many other ideas of what a community going into the 21st century would require. Although Epcot didn't meet the original vision, the park that opened in 1982 did (and still does) encompass a lot of the spirit behind Walt's original dream.

Future World brings you the latest technology, agriculture, conservation, and everything the future needs, including of course imagination. The World Showcase is similar to a world's fair. Surrounding Friendship Lake there are 11 "countries" that feature the culture, architecture, arts, people, and food you would experience if you were to visit them.

The Park Layout

Epcot is huge. The park is twice the size of the Magic Kingdom, and is essentially two parks in one: Future World and World Showcase.

As you enter the park, Spaceship Earth, the "big golf ball" that is the icon of the park, is right there to welcome you. As you go past Spaceship Earth, there is a plaza with a large fountain. Future World is divided into two sections east and west of the fountain.

Future World East. The major attraction are:

- Spaceship Earth
- Ellen's Energy Adventure
- Mission: SPACE
- Test Track
- Innoventions

Future World West. The major attraction are:

- The Seas with Nemo &Friends
- Soarin'

- Living with the Land
- Character Spot

If you go past Spaceship Earth, around the fountain, and continue to go forward, there is a bridge that leads to the World Showcase.

World Showcase. Circling the lake starting on your left, the pavilions are:

- Mexico
- Norway
- China
- Germany
- Italy
- American Adventure
- Japan
- Morocco
- France
- United Kingdom
- Canada

Guest Services. The guest relations of the park, located past Spaceship Earth on the left. Any questions you have can be addressed here. If someone in your party requires a (DAS), make sure this is your first stop.

Baby Care Center. The center is located on the World Showcase side of the Odyssey Center. You can access it from behind Test Track or off the bridge leading to World Showcase (on the left).

First Aid. First Aid is located on the World Showcase side of the Odyssey Center. You can access it from behind Test Track or off the bridge leading to World Showcase (on the left). In addition to medical concerns, First Aid accommodates adult changing needs.

ATMs. There are three ATMs in Epcot: outside the entrance, the Future World side of the bridge, and in the Germany pavilion of World Showcase.

Sensory Spots. Sensory spots are areas for taking a break and calming down, or where running free is okay. You'll find them:

- In the Cool Space behind Test Track there are misters and some room to run.
- Fountains on the bridge; although there is no shade, there are benches and little fountains designed to run through.
- The maze behind the United Kingdom pavilion. There is shade, room to run, and it's usually not a crowded area; plus, adults can sit and have a beverage.

DAS Card vs FastPass+

Trying to plan an itinerary for a family needing assistance has a couple of challenges. Everything is very personal depending on how adventurous your family is, how much you will choose to split up, etc. The lists below are designed to help you make decisions about which FastPass+ choices to make for the Epcot, compared to getting a DAS reservation. A suggested rule of thumb is to use FastPass+ for the attractions with the longest wait times. DAS is based on posted wait times, so the shorter those times are, the more you should be able to get in. Note that Epcot has a tier system with its FastPasses, which limits your option. Here are my recommendations for getting a DAS or FP+:

Tier 1 (pick 1)

- Illuminations (DAS)
- Frozen Ever After (FP+)
- Soarin' (FP+)
- Test Track (FP+)

Tier 2 (pick 2)

- Disney/Pixar Film Festival (DAS)
- Journey to Imagination with Figment (DAS)
- Epcot Character Spot (FP+)
- Living with the Land (FP+)
- The Seas with Nemo & Friends (FP+)
- Spaceship Earth (FP+)
- Turtle Talk with Crush (DAS)
- Mission: SPACE (DAS)

Future World East

The east side of Future world is more of the "thrill" side. This is where Test Track and Mission: SPACE throw you around a bit. I've also included the more centrally located Future World attraction here.

Spaceship Earth

Ride
Must Transfer / Handheld Captioning / Audio Description / Service Animals Permitted with Caution

Discover the history of communication on this slow moving, relaxing ride. It's probably how Epcot keeps it's "museum" reputation. It is definitely an educational tour. However, it is *in* the big golf ball! So the kids love that.

Sensory Impact. Dark. No worries! If there isn't a long wait, it actually makes a nice little sensory spot.

Mission: SPACE

Ride (height requirement 44")
Must Transfer / Video Captioning / No Service Animals

Pilot your mission to Mars and explore the Red Planet. There are two tracks: orange for the more adventurous, green for those easily affected by motion sickness or want a more family friendly mission. This mission pilot's around earth, pointing out landmarks that can be seen from space, then you help land the shuttle using the flight stick and buttons. There are booster seats available for smaller guests.

Sensory Impact. This can be an intense ride. Getting into the capsule can be more challenging than other "must-transfer" attractions If you have a fear of small dark spaces this can be uncomfortable.

Test Track

Ride (height requirement 40")
Single Rider / Must transfer / Video captioning / No Service Animals

Imagine you are a car designer. First you design, a car focusing on control, fuel consumption, speed, and impact, and of course make it look cool, then you get to test it on a track that simulates each element.

Sensory Impact. There are surprises that startle you, moderate in noise level (for a ride). The speed section is outdoors and very windy. Getting down into the seats can be challenging.

Innoventions

Interactive Exhibit
Accessible

Innovations is a hall designed for a few interactive displays that feel like a science museum. There are activities for all ages (think space-age coloring).

Sensory Impact. Great activity to cool off and settle down a bit.

Future World West

The west side of Future World is centered on exploring. You'll visit the seas, soar around the world, and journey through your imagination. Many of the attractions share space in their pavilions.

Epcot Character Spot

Character Meet and Greet
Accessible

Visit a variety of characters here! At press time, Baymax and Joy and Sadness (from Pixar's *Inside Out*) join Mickey and his pals. Check the MyDisneyExperience app for current characters.

The Seas with Nemo and Friends

Ride
Must Transfer to Standard Wheelchair / Handheld Captioning / Audio Description

Ride along and play with Nemo and his friends. This short ride is a fun way to enter the pavilion.

Sensory Impact. No worries.

Turtle Talk With Crush

Interactive Show
Accessible / Sign Language Available (Fridays) / Assisted Listening

Come see Crush as he answers questions about the ocean and his adventures with Squirt. The technology in this attraction is great. The kids really ask questions and Crush answers (he's animated).

Sensory Impact. No worries.

Undersea Observation Deck

Exhibit
Accessible

Thousands of sea creatures swim in these huge aquariums. This isn't in the official map (they just list the pavilion) and I wanted to emphasize how much families enjoy it. There is an entrance through the gift shop if you choose not to ride The Seas with Nemo and Friends.

Sensory Impact. It's a relaxing area where you can spend as much time as you wish enjoying the fish.

Soarin'

Ride (height requirement 40")
Must Transfer / Assisted listening / Video captioning / No service animals

Soar above the earth's finest treasures as if you are on a hang glider (although thankfully you're seated). You will feel the wind blow, smell the snow and dust, and fly past iconic buildings like the Taj Mahal and Eiffel Tower.

Sensory Impact. If you can handle heights, this is an amazing ride.

Living with the Land

Ride

Must Transfer Standard Wheelchair / Audio Description / Handheld Captioning

Board a boat and explore the ways the land works for us, and how Disney grows food in these working greenhouses (fresh produce for the pavilion restaurants is grown here).

Sensory Impact. No worries.

The Circle of Life

Film

Accessible / Assisted Listening / Video Captioning

Timon and Pumbaa present a 20-minute film about conservation.

Sensory Impact. The film can feel intense and upsetting..

Journey into Imagination

Ride

Accessible / Handheld Captioning / Audio Description

The Imagination Institute is opening their doors so guests can learn all about them. What kind of trouble will Figment get into as you take your tour? Figment is the purple dragon and a symbol of Epcot. If you remember this ride from your childhood, it is very different, and not as scary.

Sensory Impact. Odd smells, startling sounds.

World Showcase

Explore parts of the world you have never traveled to before. Every world pavilion has a Kidcot spot with an activity for kids. Dining in the World Showcase is covered in a later chapter. Here, I've included only information about attractions and shows. Not every pavilion has an attraction or a show, and so not every pavilion is listed.

As you pass the bridge into the World Showcase, you can head either right or left. It doesn't matter which way you go, as it all connects back at the beginning, but if you are trying to get to the Friendship entrance (the back gate), turn right and begin the World Showcase with the Canada pavilion.

Agent P's World Showcase Adventure

Activity

Accessible / Video Captioning

Join Phineas and Ferb in helping Agent P (their pet platypus Perry) defeat Dr. Doofenschmirtz and save the world. You will be issued a communication device or given the option to use your own smart phone on which you'll get clues to help you on your mission saving the country you are visiting..

This activity can take awhile, but it really helps you experience the country you choose, and it's a lot of fun, especially if your kids enjoy problem solving and have patience.

Sensory Impact. No worries, unless patience is a challenge. Sometimes a country is full, so don't promise a certain one until it's ready. There is no time limit; your adventure can be done at your pace.

Gran Fiesta Tour staring Donald Duck (Mexico)

Ride

Transfer to Standard Wheelchair / Handheld Captioning / Audio Description

Take a boat tour through Mexico as the Three Caballeros look for their friend Donald. He ends up in some very funny situations.

Sensory Impact. No worries.

Frozen Ever After (Norway)

Ride

Must Transfer / Handheld Captioning / Audio Description

Celebrate the music of *Frozen*. This is a beautiful ride with all of your favorite characters and music from the film.

Sensory Impact. There is a small backwards, downhill drop, it may splash you a little.

Reflections of China (China)

Film

Accessible / Assistive Listening / Handheld Captioning / Audio Description

Let this unique 14-minute film immerse you in China. It is beautiful and interesting for those who can handle Circle-Vision films. (A new film with the latest technology in seamless Circle-Vision will be introduced soon.)

Sensory Impact. You may experience motion sickness; no seating.

The American Adventure (America)

Show

Accessible / Assistive Listening / Handheld Captioning / Audio Description

A 35-minute American history lesson hosted by Benjamin Franklin and Mark Twain. This show is not all sunshine; it does refer to America's dark times such as the Civil War and slavery, but also celebrates America's accomplishments like innovation and the invention of the telephone.

Sensory Impact. No worries; large air-conditioned theater with cushioned seats.

Impressions de France (France)

Film
Accessible / Assistive Listening / Handheld Captioning / Audio Description

A beautiful score brings France to life in this 18-minute film.

Sensory Impact. No worries; fully air-conditioned theater with cushioned seats.

O! Canada (Canada)

Film
Accessible / Assistive Listening / Handheld Captioning / Audio Description

Enjoy Martin Short in a funny film highlighting all that Canada has to offer.

Sensory Impact. You may experience motion sickness; no seating.

International Gateway

If you follow the bridge there is a back entrance to Epcot. It connects to the Boardwalk and the Boardwalk resorts. There is also a boat to Disney's Hollywood Studios. You will find wheelchair, ECV, and stroller rentals here, as well as a small gift shop with necessities as well as souvenirs. If you stop on the bridge, it's a lovely photo op.

Illuminations

Fireworks
Accessible

In the middle of the lake at sunset you will notice crews in boats putting together a globe. This is the stage for Illuminations, a beautiful fireworks and laser light show that lights up World Showcase.

There are accessible viewing areas near Germany, between the UK and Canada, and on both sides of the World Showcase Plaza.

Sensory Impact. High. It's a fireworks show, so headphones are a must. The crowds are lighter and spread around the lagoon making this an easier show to watch than other fireworks shows.

Park Exit and Analysis

Unless you are staying at a Boardwalk resort, you exit Epcot near Spaceship Earth. That is where the buses and monorails are located. All monorails take you back to the TTC where you can transfer to the resort monorail or the Magic Kingdom monorail.

Epcot has a lot of treasures that get overlooked. Some of the attractions and World Showcase can take longer to experience than the quick thrills of Magic Kingdom or Hollywood Studios. Epcot is under-rated as a family park.

Coming Soon

There are two big rides coming to Epcot. The dates have not been announced, but construction has already begun.

Guardians of the Galaxy

Indoor Roller Coaster

This will be an indoor coaster with a fabulous soundtrack based on the Guardians of the Galaxy film franchise. It will be in Future World East near Mission: SPACE and the new space restaurant also coming soon!

Ratatouille

Ride

Explore a French kitchen from the perspective of our favorite chef Remy (the rat). In Disneyland Paris, this ride has fully accessible cars and uses a trackless suspension and screens for the effects. It is very popular there, but I have heard from friends that it can cause motion sickness.

CHAPTER THIRTEEN

Disney's Hollywood Studios

Hollywood Studios is experiencing a re-imagining. The focus used to be more about seeing how movies are made, now the focus is on experiencing the movies you love in a BIG way. As we await new lands and adventures there are construction areas and fewer attractions than there used to be.

The Park Layout

Hollywood Studios is the park that is most challenging to navigate on a good day. With the current construction, it is even worse. Unlike the other parks where everything flows together, there are dead ends and confusing intersections.

You enter on Hollywood Boulevard. At the end of the street you will see the Chinese Theater (just like in Hollywood). After the first block an unnamed street is on your left that will lead you to the Echo Lake and Grand Avenue areas. Two-thirds of the way up the street Sunset Boulevard is on your right, heading toward Tower of Terror and the Rock 'n' Roller Coaster. If you continue past the Chinese theater you will find Pixar Place (soon to be Toy Story Land) and Star Wars Launch Pad, plus the Little Mermaid and Disney Jr. areas.

Guest Services. Located before you enter the park on the left and after the entrance, guest services is the first building across from the gas station. Any questions you have can be addressed here. If someone in your party requires a (DAS), make sure this is your first stop.

Baby Care Center. The Baby Care Center is located with guest services in the first building across the street from the gas station.

First Aid. The First Aid Center is located is located with guest services in the first building across the street from the gas station. In addition to medical concerns, they offer a space that accommodates adult changing needs.

ATM's. There are two in Hollywood Studios Outside the entrance near the gas station, and between Center Stage and Echo Lake.

Sensory Spots. Sensory spots are areas for taking a break and calming down, or where running free is okay. The areas that were best for sensory spots are now under construction. Here are two quieter areas:

- The Launch pad has a few areas with muted lighting and air conditioning, but if your child doesn't like Star Wars imagery, I would avoid this option.
- The area of Echo Lake near the Indiana Jones Stunt Spectacular is less crowded and there are some benches.

DAS Card vs FastPass+

Trying to plan an itinerary for a family needing assistance has a couple of challenges. Everything is very personal depending on how adventurous your family is, how much you will choose to split up, etc. The lists below are designed to help you make decisions about which FastPass+ choices to make for Hollywood Studios, compared to getting a DAS reservation. A suggested rule of thumb is to use FastPass+ for the attractions with the longest wait times. DAS is based on posted wait times, so the shorter those times are, the more you should be able to get in. Note that Hollywood Studios has a tier system with its FastPasses, limiting your options. Here are my recommendation for getting a DAS or FP+:

Tier 1 (pick 1)

- Toy Story Mania (FP+)
- Beauty and the Beast Live (DAS)
- Fantasmic! (DAS)
- Rock 'n' Roller Coaster (FP+)

Tier 2 (pick 2)

- Disney Junior Live Onstage (DAS)
- Voyage of the Little Mermaid (DAS)
- Frozen Sing-along (FP+)
- Indiana Jones Epic Stunt Spectacular (DAS)
- Star Tours (FP+)
- Muppet*Vision 3D (DAS)
- Twilight Zone Tower of Terror (FP+)

Hollywood Boulevard

Walk down the street and enjoy fun shops, neon signs, and the glitz and glamour of Hollywood. Look out for actors in funny skits around town.

Echo Lake

Echo Lake celebrates a more modern(ish) period in film. *Star Wars*, *Indiana Jones*, and *Frozen* are found in these parts.

Frozen Sing-along

Show

Accessible / Sign Language (Sunday, Wednesday) / Handheld Captioning / Assistive Listening

Welcome to Arendelle. Our historians will tell you the story of Queen Elsa and Princess Anna and their adventures while you sing-along.

Sensory Impact. Kids and adults are singing along, so the volume can add up, but in a happy way. I suggest headphones.

Indiana Jones Epic Stunt Spectacular

Show

Accessible / Sign language (Sunday, Wednesday) / Handheld Captioning / Assistive Listening / Audio Description

Ever wonder how big-time stunts are done? This show explains the epic stunts of *Indiana Jones and the Temple of Doom*. The show has explosions, falling rocks, and choreographed fighting, but the humor keeps it all together.

Sensory Impact. Headphones are required, but the outdoor (under shade arena) helps the sound disperse. The action can feel intense, but the humor really does help break that up.

Jedi Training: Trials of the Temple

Interactive Show

Accessible

Younglings learn to use the Force in facing their fears. This is a special experience that trains kids 4–12 on the ways of the Force. Space is very limited. To take part, you must:

- Be at Hollywood Studios with the child at rope drop (before opening).
- After you enter the park, walk with purpose (don't run) up Hollywood Boulevard, then take the first left to Echo Lake.
- A cast member will be there with a light saber to direct you.
- Sign ups are at the Indiana Jones Outpost.

- Cast members will ask the children questions to make sure they can be safe on stage.
- Sign up for one of 15 show times, then enjoy the park until you need to report back.

As you can tell, this show is a big deal. Watching the line of kids and their fathers walk to their training with grins on their faces is fun.

Sensory Impact. Do not promise your child they will get to do this unless you have a reservation, even if you are first in line. Fighting Darth Vadar can be scary (even if they remind you it's to face your fears and he's not real).

Star Tours: The Adventure Continues

Ride (height restriction 40")
Standard Wheelchair Then Transfer / Handheld Captioning / Video captioning

Take in a 3D film that moves like a flight simulator takes you on different adventures through the *Star Wars* universe.

Sensory Impact. This ride throws you around quite a bit. There are loud explosions and tense moments.

Grand Avenue

Representing modern Los Angeles, there are façades with fun windows and spots for photo ops while you sip on your beer from the Baseline Tap House. This is a nice transition area as Toy Story Land and Galaxy's Edge (Star Wars Land) open in the future.

Muppet*Vision 3D

3D Film
Accessible / Assisted Listening / Handheld Captioning / Video Captioning / Audio Description

Muppet Labs with Professor Honeydew are busy creating 3D effects for films with hysterical shenanigans as only the Muppets can do.

Sensory Impact. There are some explosions, but they are based in humor. My family has an easier time with these explosions because they are silly and not based in violence. However, headphones still help with the noise.

Pixar Place

Join your *Toy Story* friends for a carnival. Green army men might ask you to drop and give them 20 (push-ups, of course).

Toy Story Mania

3D Interactive Ride
Standard Wheelchair / Video Captioning / Audio Description

Andy's toys set up a carnival in his room. Enjoy games and fun while competing with your family.

Sensory Impact. Be prepared to manage expectations if it's hard to lose.

Animation Courtyard

This area is all about Walt Disney's beginnings in the movies: animation.

Walt Disney Presents

Exhibit
Accessible / Reflective Captioning / Assisted Listening / Audio Description / Handheld Captioning

Walk through exhibits and see a film about Walt Disney and his amazing career and legacy.

Sensory Impact. No worries.

Voyage of the Little Mermaid

Live Performance
Accessible / Reflective Captioning / Assisted Listening / Audio Description

Under the Sea is where the party is. Experience this fun show highlighting the beautiful music of *The Little Mermaid.*

Sensory Impact. Moderate. Intense storylines with bubbles and some mild effects.

Star Wars Launch Bay

Exhibit, Meet and Greet
Accessible / Reflective Captioning / Assisted Listening / Audio Description / Handheld Captioning

Experience all things *Star Wars* with real movie props and costumes, and meet Chewbacca, BB-8, and Kylo Ren. This is a large space with many things for *Star Wars* fans to enjoy at their leisure.

Sensory Impact. Chewbacca, BB-8, and Kylo Ren are behind doors, so if you don't want to see them you won't. BB-8 doesn't roll around. He is up on a pedestal. He does talk to you and move his head.

Disney Junior Live!

Exhibit, Meet and Greet
Accessible / Assisted Listening / Video Captioning / Audio Description / Handheld Captioning

Sing, dance, and play with your favorite characters from Disney Junior.

Sensory Impact. Kids singing, seating on the floor

Sunset Boulevard

Stroll down Sunset Boulevard for action and laughs.

Beauty and the Beast

Live Show
Accessible / Reflective Captioning / Assisted Listening / Audio Description / Handheld Captioning / Video Captioning

"A tale as old as time" told on stage in the show that inspired the Broadway hit.

Sensory Impact. Bench seating in shaded outdoors.

Rock 'n' Roller Coaster

Roller Coaster (height restriction 40")
Single Rider / Must Transfer Twice

Aerosmith is late for a concert and they invited you, so the limo will get through LA traffic super fast.

Sensory Impact. Looping rollercoaster with a high-speed start. Very loud soundtrack. This is for thrill seekers. Ben needs me to cover his ears for the extra loud start.

Twilight Zone Tower of Terror

Thrill Ride (height restriction 40")
Single Rider / Must Transfer Twice

An old abandoned hotel shares its harrowing story about its last guests while the elevator loses control.

Sensory Impact. Scary theme, ride drops, fear of heights.

Fantasmic!

Live Show
Accessible / Assisted Listening / Audio Description / Handheld Captioning

Mickey's dreams are larger than life as he battles Disney villians.

When exiting the show the crowd is guided to a side exit. This is great if you are ready to leave the park, but if you need to meet the rest of your family, break away before you find yourself outside the gates.

Sensory Impact. The themes are frightening and the show is large with fire and water sprays. The volume isn't bad because of the venue. The theater is a large amphitheater with no cover in case of rain.

Star Wars: A Galactic Spectacular

Fireworks
Accessible

You've never experienced *Star Wars* like this. A fabulous laser projection fireworks show that incorporates clips, music, and characters from the entire saga projected on the Chinese Theater.

Sensory Impact. It's a fireworks show, so headphones are a must.

Park Analysis

You can often hear Hollywood Studios referred to as a half-day park. As the park exists right now, I agree. If you are a fireworks family, I suggest this park after lunch and naps. If you don't have park hoppers, come in the morning (get on some rides and sign up for Jedi Training, then there is a lot of time for lunch and naps before you come back). I wouldn't skip this park, especially if you love *Star Wars*.

Coming Soon

Andy's friends, the first ride starring Mickey and Minnie Mouse, and a galaxy full of adventure will be arriving at Hollywood Studios soon. Because these areas have not opened, I do not have information about accessibility.

Mickey and Minnie Runaway Railway

Mickey and Minnie will star in their first-ever ride. You will step through a movie screen and find yourself in a cartoon with Mickey and his friends on a zany adventure just like the Mickey shorts airing on the Disney Channel.

Toy Story Land

(Coming summer 2018.) Andy is using his toys and imagination building a fabulous park in his backyard. The new attractions in this land will include Slinky Dog Dash, a mild roller coaster, and Alien Swirling Saucers, a family-friendly ride.

Galaxy's Edge

(Coming summer 2019.) Otherwise known as Star Wars Land, Galaxy's Edge is its official name. This is a fully immersive area of the park designed to transport you into a world where you can fly the *Millennium Falcon*, mingle with aliens and droids, and enjoy all things Star Wars.

CHAPTER FOURTEEN

Disney's Animal Kingdom

Bambi, Baloo, Pumba, are all classic Disney characters, but did you know about Peri the squirrel and the other True-Life Adventure shows that highlight the majesty of the animal kingdom? Walt Disney had a respect and love for nature, and Disney's Animal Kingdom combines that love with his genius in entertainment to create an amazing park!

The Park Layout

Animal Kingdom has five sections, each connected like the lands in the Magic Kingdom. After you enter, you head toward the Tree of Life and you are on Discovery Island. From there you can take a trail to any of the lands:

- Africa
- Asia
- DinoLand USA
- Pandora: Land of Avatar

Guest Services. On the left the building is divided so you can visit from outside the park or inside. Any questions you have can be addressed here. If someone in your party requires a (DAS), make sure this is your first stop.

Baby Care Center. The center is located on Discovery Island near the entrance to Africa.

First Aid. First Aid is located on Discovery Island near the entrance to Africa. In addition to medical concerns they offer a space that accommodates adult changing needs.

ATMs. There are two in Animal Kingdom: inside the entrance on the right and in DinoLand USA.

Sensory Spots. Sensory spots are areas that are good for taking a break and calming down, or an area where running free is okay. This park works exceptionally well for that!

- Boneyard.

- Rafiki's Planet Watch.
- Outside the DINOSAUR ride.
- There are many gardens and spots to see animals that work well for a break. As you get closer to the Tree of Life, you can see just how amazing it is. The animal carvings that create the trunk, branches, and even roots look as if they grew that way. Stay and discover animals, gardens where you can explore more of the tree, and fun animals.

DAS Card vs FastPass+

Trying to plan an itinerary for a family needing assistance has a couple of challenges. Everything is very personal depending on how adventurous your family is, how much you will choose to split up, etc. The lists below are designed to help you make decisions about which FastPass+ choices to make for Animal Kingdom, compared to getting a DAS reservation. A suggested rule of thumb is to use FastPass+ for the attractions with the longest wait times. DAS is based on posted wait times, so the shorter those times are, the more you should be able to get in. Here are my recommendation for getting a DAS or FP+:

Tip: Flight of Passage FastPasses are very hard to get. I encourage trying the moment you are eligible. The average wait time is 3 hours, and often longer.

DAS

- DINOSAUR
- Festival of the Lion King
- Finding Nemo The Musical
- It's tough to be a Bug!
- Adventurers Outpost Meet Mickey and Minnie
- Primeval Whirl
- Na'vi River Journey

FP+

- Avatar Flight of Passage
- Expedition Everest
- Kali River Rapids
- Kilimanjaro Safaris

Discovery Island

Discovery Island is the first "land" you come to after entering the park.

Wilderness Explorers

Interactive Adventure
Accessible

Join the Wilderness Explorers and earn badges by completing challenges and learning about the wildlife throughout the park. Additional Wilderness Explorer stations are in Africa, Asia, Rafiki's Planet, and DinoLand USA.

Sensory Impact. Completing your Wilderness Adventure badges can help create interest in the park and be a lot of fun.

It's Tough to Be a Bug!

4D Film
Accessible / Assisted Listening / Audio Description / Reflective captioning / Handheld Captioning / Service Animals with Caution

Flick from Pixar's *A Bug's Life* wants to help you understand the world from a bug's perspective.

Sensory Impact. This attraction is frightening, has odd smells, pokes you, is loud, and the entrance has a low ceiling that feels very cramped and extra crowded. I do not recommend this attraction for those with sensory needs. I have friends that had to leave even with typically developing children.

Discovery Island Trails

Walking Trail
Accessible

These trails let you get a little closer to the animal carvings on the Tree of Life. It's also a pretty good place to run around a bit or get fun photos!

Adventures Outpost

Character Meet and Greet
Accessible

Meet Mickey and Minnie in their adventure outfits.

Pandora: The World of Avatar

Pandora is an immersive experience set in the fictional world of Pandora from the James Cameron film Avatar. It is a beautiful land that focuses on conservation (just like Animal Kingdom always has) and fits well in the park. It has areas to explore, fun new things to eat, and amazing landscape that is unique and beautiful during the day and spectacularly lit at night. Even if you haven't seen film, you will still enjoy this area.

Sensory Impact. In order to create an immersive world there are sounds and experiences you've never encountered before. Some of the sounds (think cicadas) can be loud. The landa is not flat. There are many hills and little areas with a few steps here and there that make it hard to navigate with a push wheelchair. Scooters are fine.

Na'vi River Journey

Dark Ride
FastPass+/ must transfer/ handheld captioning/ audio description

See the world of Pandora as the Na'vi do in a stunning journey through a bioluminescent rainforest. You will discover new creatures, plants, and beauty while searching for the Shaman of Songs.

Sensory Impact. This is a calm restful ride with enough cool lighting to keep it from being too dark.

Avatar Flight of Passage

Thrill Ride
FastPass+/ height restriction 44"/ Must transfer to standard wheelchair/ assistive listening/ video captioning/ audio description
Strobe lights; fear of hights

Fly on the back of a mountain banshee and experience the exhilarating world of Pandora with its breathtaking landscapes and thrilling adventure.

Any age group will love this ride, but it does not easily accommodate everyone, limiting the audience that can enjoy it. It is built like a motorcycle-ride video game, so you need to slide onto it from behind. It does adjust a little and pumps up higher for people in wheelchairs to board. It is also unforgiving if you are very tall, larger, or even if you work out a lot and have big calves. Because of the restrictions, there is a seat in front that cast Mmembers will assist you with to see if you can ride. Some people will know right away, others are a maybe. If you are a maybe, go for it. The inside seats move and adjust some, the outside seat doesn't. Even the queue area is not wheelchair friendly. It is pretty steep and very long.

If you are seizure prone, while you are boarding look forward, do not look down at the seat. If you have anxiety, the boarding process can take a few minutes; try to breathe and relax while waiting.

The visors for 3D viewing are large. My daughter used a headband to go over the visor and hold it in place.

Sensory Impact. High. There are intense moments, strange smells, and drops from extreme heights. It is not loud.

Africa

Festival of the Lion King

Live Show

Accessible / Assisted Listening / Audio Description / Reflective Captioning / Handheld Captioning / Sign Language (Tuesdays and Saturdays)

Timon wants you to experience Africa through his story in *The Lion King*. The dancing, singing, fantastic costuming, and jokes entertain everyone.

Sensory Impact. As with any live performance, it can be a little loud. Bring headphones. There is not an easy way to exit this theater. If you think you may need help, speak to a cast member before the show.

Kilimanjaro Safaris

Safari Ride

Standard Wheelchair / Assisted Listening / Video Captioning / Service Animals with Caution

Take a safari through the African wildlife preserve. See giraffes, elephants, lions, and many other animals in a natural setting.

Sensory Impact. It's a bumpy ride, and sometimes it's harder to see the animal you are looking for. Staying seated is challenging, but mandatory.

Gorilla Falls Exploration Trail

Walking Trail

Accessible / Audio Description

Walk through a tropical jungle and see gorillas, hippos, and exotic birds.

Sensory Impact. No worries sensory spot.

Wildlife Express Train

Train Ride

Accessible / Assisted Listening / Handheld Captioning

This is the train to Rafiki's Planet Watch. On the way you will see behind the scenes of where the animals are taken care of.

Sensory Impact. No worries

Rafiki's Planet Watch

Learn about conservation and how all of the animals are taken care; plus, this is where you get to pet some animals.

Habitat Habit

Walking Trail

Accessible

An outdoor trail with cotton–topped tamarin monkeys and many ideas on how to keep their habitat healthy.

Sensory Impact. No worries.

Conservation Station

Exhibit, Films
Sensory Friendly

This is a cool building with short films, rest areas, and most importantly, veterinarian offices. You can see the veterinarians helping the animals that need care.

Sensory Impact. No worries.

Affection Section

Petting Zoo
Standard Wheelchair / No Service Animals

Visit with friendly domesticated animals including breeds you don't get to see many places.

Sensory Impact. No worries

Asia

Mysterious lands with beautiful tigers, rapids, and Mt. Everest lead you to fabulous adventures.

Flights of Wonder

Show
Accessible / Assisted Listening / Sign Language (Tuesdays and Saturdays)

Birds are graceful, beautiful...and funny. This is a wonderful show that teaches about birds as well as entertains all ages.

Sensory Impact. Funny and not scary, unless someone in your group has a fear of birds.

Maharajah Jungle Trek

Walking Trail
Accessible / Audio description / Service Animals (with caution in aviary section)

Follow the trail to find tigers, bats, and Komodo dragons.

Sensory Impact. no worries

Kali River Rapids

Water Ride (height restriction 38")
Must Transfer / No Service Animals

As you travel the rough waters, there are dips and water sprays that help ensure you will get drenched. Have ziplock bags for electronics. Shoes are required. If you are worried about wet socks, it won't hurt to have extras, or easy-to-pack flip-flops or water shoes.

Sensory Impact. It can feel a little dangerous, and you will get wet.

Expedition Everest

Roller Coaster (height restriction 44")
Single Rider / Must transfer / No Service Animals

A speeding train takes you up the mountain, and then you discover the Yeti is near. You go speeding backwards and see him from afar; and, if you keep an eye peeled, close up, too.

Sensory Impact. This i roller-coaster thrill ride has some scary themes and a giant (but immobile) monster. The smooth technology makes it less noisy, but some may feel better with headphones. Ben likes us to enter the car first to ensure he doesn't ride under the Yeti.

DinoLand U.S.A.

From awesome to silly, DinoLand U.S.A. covers every entertainment angle of dinosaurs.

The Boneyard

Playground
Accessible

Enter this dinosaur dig to explore in tunnels, climb ,and slide down multiple layers of the work site.

Sensory Impact. No worries. Sand is contained.

Finding Nemo: The Musical

Live Show
Accessible / Assisted Listening / Reflective Captioning / Sign Language (Tuesdays and Saturdays) / Audio Description

Help find Nemo with original songs and the characters you love as fantastic puppets. The storyline is a condensed version of the movie.

Sensory Impact. The music can be strong; headphones are a good idea. Seating is wooden benches with backs.

Primeval Whirl

Thrill Ride (height restriction 48")
Must Transfer / No Service Animals

This time machine is spinning and dropping you through time to avoid "the end of the world." Think of a traveling carnival thrill ride.

Sensory Impact. There are a lot of ups and downs, jerking around and spinning. It's not very loud.

TriceraTop Spin

Ride
Standard Wheeelchair

Fly just like Dumbo, except in a cute extinct animal.

Sensory Impact. No worries.

DINOSAUR

Dark Ride (height restriction 40")
Must transfer / Assisted Listening / Video Captioning / No Service Animals

Travel back in time to save a dinosaur from extinction, and hope everything goes smoothly.

Sensory Impact. Headphones, intense theme, severe jerking and motion.

Park Analysis

Animal Kingdom is a beautiful park with enough surprises and thrills to keep all guests happy. The authenticity is striking, although it does make it more challenging with wheelchairs. Look carefully at signs; everything blends together so seamlessly that things can be easy to miss.

The addition of a glowing Pandora is another reason to not to miss Animal Kingdom at night. The lighting is vibrant and beautiful, there is dancing, DJ parties, and everything is even more alive. I suggest arriving for an early dinner doing the safari and animal trails and maybe a show, then as the sun sets experience the entertainment and rides at night.

CHAPTER FIFTEEN

Time to Eat

Dining is an important piece of your vacation. Meals can also be a memorable part of the experience. At Disney there are a lot of choices.

Dining Experiences

- *Character Meals.* The characters come around and visit guests at the table. Many character meals are buffets. This can be a great way to visit with characters without as much pressure or lines. For character meals, I recommend an advanced dining reservation (ADR) booked as early as possible.
- *Table service.* A sit down or buffet restaurant. Most have fun or interesting themes like Sci Fi Dine In at Hollywood Studios or Coral Reef in Epcot. The prices range from expensive to very expensive.
- *Quick Service.* Think fast food, either a counter or a type of food court where you go to stations for different choices, then pay a cashier.
- *Kiosks and Food Carts.* Sprinkled throughout the resort there are goodies on carts ranging from ice cream to full meals, though not a lot of seating.
- *Food Trucks.* Disney Springs has food trucks.
- *Refillable Mug.* You can refill the mug with hot or cold beverages during the length of your stay at any Disney property hotel.

Disney Dining Plan

If you are staying at a Disney resort (not Shades of Green, the Swan, or the Dolphin) and purchase the Magic Your Way package, there are a few dining plans that allow you to pay for your dining (minus gratuity or alcohol) before you even arrive at Disney World. The cost is based on how many nights you stay, and the food is discounted.

There are times when the Disney Dining Plan is offered free if you have a full-price room. Very often that is a great deal (sometimes a discounted room is worth more, so check the math).

All of the plans are for each day for the length of your stay, for each member of your party over 2 years old. Anything you don't eat one day carries over to the next. Or, you can eat more than the daily formula and have less available at the end. All credits expire at midnight the last day of your stay.

A few frequently asked questions about the Disney Dining Plan:

- Can I eat at Cinderella Castle? Yes, but you use 2 meal credits per person.
- Are gratuities included? No, except at Cinderella's Royal Table, dinner shows like Hoop De Doo, and room service.
- Are dinner shows included? Yes, But Mickey's Backyard BBQ is 2 meal credits per person.
- How about character meals? Yes, if you have table service credits.
- What if we have food allergies? When you are booking the reservation tell the operator about your allergy. Also tell the server or manager at the restaurant.
- Can a buffet work with a food allergy? Yes. I've seen a chef at a buffet change to a fresh pan just for a guest with an egg allergy. Foods are labeled at the buffets, but I suggest speaking with a manager to make sure they are extra vigilant.
- If I'm on the deluxe plan, do we each have to order an appetizer and dessert? No, and remember the gratuity isn't included, so don't order food just because you can.

Special tips for Disney Dining plans:

- If you are dining with another family using a dining plan. be sure to let the server know who belongs to which bill.
- At table service and character dining, children 3–9 must use the children's menu if there is one.
- Guests older than 9 may choose from the children's menu if they would like.

Mobile Orders

Mobile ordering is similar to a FastPass for quick service meals. You skip the lines for ordering and paying for your order. You order and pay for the meal using the MyDisneyExperience App on your phone. As you are getting your family seated, you will be notified on your phone when your meal is ready.

I can't recommend this new service enough. It has made eating in quick service locations much more relaxing and easy to navigate. However, there are a few things you need to know. Currently, the Disney Dining Plan, gift cards, and cash can't be used to order. You will ne debit card available even if you have been using credit for purchases.

Here are some brief overviews of table-service rest meals in the theme parks and at the resort hotels:

Magic Kingdom

Cinderella's Royal Table

Dining in Cinderella's Castle overlooking Fantasyland is as magical as it sounds. First you enter the castle and have a photo with your hostess, Cinderella, then upstairs in the dining room a few of her princess friends come around and meet you at your table. Every detail makes this royal meal a memory to treasure.

Don't promise this will happen until you have the reservation. Also, if you have a non-princess person that will spoil the magic, why force it. It's an expensive meal for someone who will not appreciate it. Divide and conquer when possible.

If it fits in your budget, every princess should experience Cinderella Castle at least once. One magical morning when my daughter, Meg, was eight, we made an early appointment for Bibbidi Bobbidi Boutique, then we had a girls' breakfast in the castle. She still remembers it as an amazing day.

Sensory Impact. There is a little "show" where everyone waves their magic wands, but the sensory issues are minimal.

The Crystal Palace

Winnie the Pooh and friends are bouncing around the dining room to meet with all of their friends. A quiet, sunshine-filled restaurant makes for a lovely meal that makes even Eeyore smile.

We always enjoy meals at the Crystal Palace. There is just such a sweetness to Pooh, and the little kids have smiles that light up the room when they see their friends from the Hundred Acre Woods have come to say hello.

Sensory Impact. Crystal Palace has a buffet, so there are a lot of food options, and the restaurant is quiet. No worries!

Be Our Guest

Enter Beast's Castle and enjoy your surroundings as much as the food. Be Our Guest has an interesting set up. During lunch and breakfast, this is a quick-service restaurant, and at dinner it transforms to table service where Beast is the host. He waits in the library to take pictures with you as you leave.

reakfast and lunch you arrive and tell the host you are there. They direct you to a line where you place your order on a large touch screen. en you receive an enchanted rose and find your own table. The rose helps the server locate your table and bring your food to you on a cart, "as if by magic." There are three rooms available: the Grand Ballroom, the Rose Gallery, and the West Wing. The rooms look just like those in the animated classic *Beauty and the Beast*.

For dinner, from 4 until park close, the castle transforms into a table-service restaurant. A cast member will seat you, a server will come to the table to take your order, and the lighting is dimmed. Overall, it is a calmer, quieter space. As a bonus for adults, beer and wine are on the menu.

Sensory Impact. The West Wing in the movie was a forbidden area; here in the restaurant, it can be scary, with a thunderstorm every 15 minutes or so. My recommendation is to sit in the Rose Gallery. It is a smaller room with less noise. If the Rose Gallery is full, stick to the right side of the Grand Ballroom and you never have to see the West Wing, but feel free to get up and check it out. Beast is very large and can be intimidating. If he is too scary, it is easy to skip the photo op.

Jungle Navigation Co. Ltd.

If you love the humor of the Jungle Cruise and great food, you've found the right place. The décor and "story" are reminiscent of the classic ride. The atmosphere is light, but more adult than the character meals.

Sensory Impact. Check out the menu before you make this reservation. There might be more adventure than a picky eater is ready for (but they do have some items for the timid).

Liberty Tree Tavern

Welcome to a colonial tavern with décor and a menu to match its colonial theme. A pre-determined menu is served family style for dinner, and at lunch there is a menu with traditional choices. Beer and wine are now available.

Sensory Impact. This location is accessible, but not accessible friendly; there are a lot of steps.

Diamond Horseshow

Family-style BBQ with salad and a choice of entree's fixed country style, and drinks and brownies for dessert.

Sensory Impact. Loud, long tables in a large open hall. I don't recommend it.

The Plaza Restaurant

This is a table-service restaurant that does not accept reservations. You walk up and ask for a table. The food is simple and good, a nice option if you decide quick service just won't work that day.

Sensory Impact. The seating is old-fashioned ice cream tables, and the dining room is attached to an ice cream parlor, so if you want to discourage ice cream, this may not be the spot for you.

Tony's Town Square Restaurant

The romance of *Lady and the Tramp* is everywhere in this traditional Italian restaurant. There are certainly more exciting places to eat, but the *Lady and the Tramp* art is charming and the food is safe for picky eaters.

Sensory Impact. Ask to sit in the traditional dining room and not the enclosed patio. Although the patio has nice windows looking out onto Main Street, it is a concrete floor with rod iron chairs, and it's not quiet. Also, *Lady and the Tramp* plays in the lobby. I recommend frontloading everyone because they won't get to see it all before you have to eat.

Epcot

The Garden Grill (The Land)

Chip and Dale want to show off what they have been growing in their garden, so they want you to join them and their friends for a meal. Pluto and Mickey are also there to meet with guests at their tables.

Some of the food served in the Garden Grill was actually grown in Living with the Land below the restaurant, and some of the tables revolve, giving you a view of the ride below.

Sensory Impact. Not all of the tables revolve. If a family member will be sensitive to that, let the host know when you arrive.

Akershus Royal Banquet Hall (Norway)

If you couldn't get a table at Cinderella's Royal Table, you have a chance at dining with princesses here. This is a Norwegian buffet and there are some American kid items as well. This was a situation where my old kids ate kids meal food, because they couldn't do the traditional meals.

The princesses that come to your table to talk with you include Snow White, Aurora, and Ariel (all subject to change), but not Anna or Elsa. This can be confusing since you are right next to the Frozen Ever After ride. Anna and Elsa are in the Norway pavilion at their Sommerhus.

Sensory Impact. The first thing to do is check the menu and make sure there are options for your family. Then know that there is a little parade of kids that isn't very loud and of course participation is voluntary.

Coral Reef Restaurant (The Living Seas)

The restaurant is surrounded by beautiful aquariums and a nice atmosphere, and you can even see the divers. This is a wonderful space for a meal. Although the menu is mostly fish, there is chicken and steak, and plenty of kids' options as well.

Sensory Impact. They might be so enthralled with the sea turtles swimming by that they forget to eat. But no other worries.

Biergarten Restaurant (Germany)

A party is always happening in a Biergarten, and this one has live music and sing alongs. The food is traditional German.

Sensory Impact. This is a tough one. Headphones can help with the music. But the seating is long benches and different parties all sitting together. There are probably better options, and the beer and pretzels are also sold in the kiosk outside.

Chefs de France (France)

This lovely restaurant has French food and wines in a beautiful café with windows looking out on to the pavilion.

Sensory Impact. No worries.

La Hacienda de San Angel (Mexico)

This traditional Mexican restaurant offers waterfront dining, with full meals and plenty of kids' options.

Sensory Impact. Make sure the kids know this is not the restaurant inside the large temple.

Le Cellier Steakhouse (Canada)

Le Cellier is a beautiful stone restaurant with exquisite food and a price to match. You don't find as many families here as you do couples.

Sensory Impact. No worries.

Monsieur Paul (France)

Monsieur Paul is on the second floor above Les Chefs de France, with great views of the World Showcase.

Sensory Impact. There is a kids' menu, but it will also seem formal.

Nine Dragons Restaurant (China)

Nine Dragons is a traditional Chinese restaurant with selections from several regions of China.

Sensory Impact. No kids' menu.

Restaurant Marrakesh (Morocco)

Not only is the restaurant beautiful, but the entertainment is as well. Belly dancers perform while you enjoy delicacies from the Middle East.

Sensory Impact. No worries, plus there are chicken tenders on the menu.

Rose and Crown Dining Room (United Kingdom)

Fish and chips and other British favorites are served up in a traditional way—next to a pub. The kids' choices are limited (the Brits fry fish, not chicken).

Sensory Impact. Headphones might be necessary at busy times.

San Angel Inn Restaurante (Mexico)

Inside the large Mayan temple there is a beautiful restaurant that feels like you are dining outside in the moonlight, but you are completely comfortable in air conditioning. This restaurant also overlooks the boats heading into the Gran Fiesta Tour. The menu includes traditional Mexican food, and the kids' menu includes tacos and quesadillas.

Sensory Impact. No worries.

Spice Road Table (Morocco)

There isn't a prettier spot to eat in Epcot. The beautiful tiles and the restaurant's waterfront location are amazing. The menu has small bites and full entrees, but no specific kids' selections.

Sensory Impact. Spicy food with no kid options. The dining is outside in shade.

Teppan Edo (Japan)

A cool dining experience where your favorite Japanese foods are cooked right in front of you. There are several menu choices and add-ons, plus a few kids' entrées.

Sensory Impact. They cook *on* the table.

Tokyo Dining (Japan)

Traditional Japanese food, including sushi. The kids' selections include spring rolls and choices for the less adventurous. The only question is, are you good at chopsticks? If you time your dinner right, there's a perfect view of IllumiNations from the patio.

Sensory Input. No worries.

Tutto Italia Ristorante (Italy)

Everyone's favorite Italian meals can be found here, including vegetarian and kids' entrees. There is patio seating and in a dining room furnished just as you would expect, with murals of Italy on the wall.

Sensory Impact. No worries!

Via Napoli Ristorante e Pizzeria (Italy)

Stone oven-cooked authentic pizza. For those used to "American pizza," it could seem *too* authentic.

Sensory Impact. The acoustics are not friendly; it is a loud space. Also, you might need to explain in advance that the pizza is different from the kind typically available here.

Disney's Hollywood Studios

Hollywood and Vine

At the buffet breakfast, Jake the Pirate, Doc McStuffins, and other Disney Jr. friends stop by for table-side meet and greets. A fun morning for the pre-school set. For lunch and dinner the buffet becomes a beach party, Halloween party, Hollywood glamour party, and other fun soirées. Mickey, Minnie, Goofy, Donald, and Daisy are in costumes to fit the theme.

Sensory Impact. The breakfast is louder than lunch and dinner because the little guys get very excited.

50's Prime Time Café

The servers act like typical "moms" from the 1950s, including telling you to finish your veggies. Each table is set up to look like a 50's kitchen, with a black-and-white TV on the table playing clips of classic TV shows. The menu includes American classics like fried chicken and meatloaf.

Sensory Impact. The servers interact with the guests more than you're used to. Ours completely understood that she needed to tone it down and we were fine, plus Ben zoned out to watch the TV. So, good and bad. The dividers that set the scene of the "kitchens" helps keep the volume at a nice level.

The Hollywood Brown Derby

The Brown Derby is modeled after the iconic restaurant of the same name in Hollywood. Caricatures of movie stars are on the walls. It feels so real you'll start looking for Gene Kelly or Elizabeth Taylor to arrive. The food is fancy and foodies will love it, but there are still options on the kids' menu.

Sensory Impact. No worries!

Baseline Tap House

Craft beer and upscale bar snacks are on tap. Perfect for hanging out on Grand Avenue for some people watching. Disney Dining Plan not accepted.

Mama Melrose's Ristorante Italiano

Sometimes the familiar can be comforting when you travel. Mama Melrose's isn't a chain you will recognize, but the menu and décor will feel familiar if you eat at Italian restaurants at home.

Sensory Impact. No worries!

Sci-Fi Dine-In Theater

Remember the drive in theaters? Or maybe you never had the chance to experience them. Now you can. The inside looks like a night sky, with convertibles parked in lines, all facing a huge movie screen. The "films" are clips from classic black-and-white sci-fi movies. The only reason you know it isn't real is that the food is better than what's typically served at a concession stand.

This really is a cool concept, but I didn't like the way it forces everyone to watch a screen while sitting side by side, or even in different "rows". Dinner is when I look forward to having the time to talk about everyone's favorite part of the day, and it's just not possible here.

Sensory Impact. Unique doesn't always work out well for everyone. The "car" seating forces everyone to sit facing the screen, and it is very dark. Keeping track of everyone's needs can be challenging.

Animal Kingdom

Tusker House

Tusker House offers a bountiful buffet with a nice selection of American foods and some interesting and tasty African delicacies.

Sensory Impact. There are smaller dining rooms that are often quieter. Don't hesitate to ask the server for the quietest space available. Sometimes you need headphones, but not always.

Rainforest Café

Rainforest Café is a popular chain, with two locations at WDW: Animal Kingdom and Disney Springs. The restaurant will transport you into the rainforests and during your meal the weather will mimic that of a tropical rainforest, complete with simulated rain and thunderstorms. The menu is standard fare and shouldn't cause any concerns, despite the exotic theme.

Sensory Impact. There is a lot going on, and the thunderstorms could be troubling.

Yak and Yeti

The menu is a mix of different Asian dishes, nothing overly exotic, but good. It's a well-themed restaurant, as well, with lots to look at.

Sensory Impact. No worries.

Tiffins

Fine dining at its most exotic. The entrées are quite intimidating, but the kids menu has choices for picky eaters. Guests of any age can order from the kids menu.

Sensory Impact. No worries.

Resort Character Dining

There are many choices for dining at the various resorts. The table-service dining options are all accessible, sensory friendly, and rarely need an urgent reservation. Character meals and dinner shows are something different, and do require advance planning. They include:

1900 Park Fare (Grand Floridian)

Breakfast with Mary Poppins is practically perfect, and she is joined by characters from *Alice in Wonderland*, Mad Hatter, Winnie the Pooh, and Tigger. At dinner, Cinderella and Prince Charming welcome you to a feast with beef, chicken, seafood, and pasta dishes. There is a kid friendly menu. "Guest" characters often appear, like Cinderella's stepsisters and Lady Tremaine.

Sensory Impact. No worries, unless meeting some villains will be upsetting.

Cape May Café (Beach Club)

Traditional breakfast buffet with Mickey, Minnie, Donald, and Goofy. Cape May is open for lunch and dinner, serving a buffet with seafood and American fare, but the characters only visit during breakfast.

Sensory Impact. No worries!

Chef Mickey's (Contemporary)

Eat all you want with Mickey, Donald, Pluto, Goofy, and Minnie as the monorail goes over your head.

Sensory Impact. There is a lot going on, and the acoustics aren't great. Headphones.

'Ohana (Polynesian)

'Ohana means family,and Stitch, Lilo, Mickey, and Pluto want to welcome you to theirs. All of the choices are served directly at your table, and you may ask for seconds (and thirds).

Sensory Impact. Most of the time there are no worries, but then they hand out maracas for a parade following Stitch around around the room (if you want to). During this activity, it gets a little loud.

Spirit of Aloha (Polynesian)

A luau with dancing and an all-you-can-eat buffet, including soft drinks, coffee, beer, and wine, plus specialty cocktails for an extra charge.

Sensory Impact. There is fire and other stunts, plus a live performance. Headphones.

Trattoria al Forno (Boardwalk)

Breakfast is hosted by Rapunzel, Flynn Rider, Ariel, and Prince Eric. Enjoy Mickey waffles or other fun choices from a pre-set menu. Specialty and alcoholic beverages are additional.

Sensory Impact. No worries.

Hoop Dee Doo Revue (Fort Wilderness)

An all-you-can-eat country buffet plus beer, sangria, and soft drinks.

Sensory Impact. With any live performance, I recommend headphones.

Mickey's Backyard BBQ (Fort Wilderness)

Mickey, Minnie, Goofy, Chip, and Dale host a country-western show with rope tricks, a band, line dancing, and fun! This dinner show is the most interactive, and allows you to do more than just watch.

Sensory Impact. With any live performance, I recommend headphones.

SECTION THREE

Everything Else in the World

There's More to Walt Disney World Than Theme Parks

CHAPTER SIXTEEN

Water Parks

There are two water parks to choose from: Typhoon Lagoon and Blizzard Beach. Both of them have exciting flume and raft rides, lazy rivers, and kids water play areas with toddler-sized activities. Neither water park is very easy for guests with mobility or developmental disabilities. Many of the attractions require long lines up steps to get to the top of the slides. There is no FP+ at the water parks, and there are no back entrances for those with DAS passes, either. You are rarely allowed to wait at the end for your family, or ride with them. A lot of independence is required.

Water parks can be extra challenging for people with disabilities. I often think you are better off spending the day at the resort pool. However, if I had to choose between Typhoon Lagoon and Blizzard Beach, I lean toward Blizzard. The toddler and kids areas have more to offer and the décor requires less sand.

Typhoon Lagoon

A typhoon came through and changed the village that rests on the lagoon forever. There's even a shrimp boat stuck up on a mountain. That mountain tries and tries to break it loose with a geyser every half hour, but so far the shrimp boat is still stuck there.

Sensory Impact. The theme is islands, and with islands come sand. There are long lines, with no policies for people with disabilities to circumvent those lines.

Blizzard Beach

A freak snowstorm has hit the island and everything looks like a Christmas celebration instead of a luau. There's even a ski lift that will take you up to the Summit Plummet, a super-intense water ride.

Sensory Impact. The same reservations apply for Blizzard Beach as they do for Typhoon Lagoon, though here you'll have less sand to contend with.

CHAPTER SEVENTEEN

Disney Springs

Disney Springs is an outdoor entertainment complex featuring Disney-themed and upscale shopping, many restaurants, a theater, huge arcade called DisneyQuest, a bowling alley, and other activities.

Disney Springs is a great place to spend the evening on the day you arrive, or anytime you have some unscheduled hours to fill.

Layout

Disney Springs consists of four different areas:

- The Marketplace has Disney-themed shops and some dining, including the Rainforest Café, T-Rex (similar to Rainforest Café, but with a dinosaur theme), and Earl of Sandwich
- The Town Center is where you'll find the new high-end retail outlets, including LaCoste, Tommy Bahama, Oakey, and many others.
- The Landing has world-class dining.
- The West Side is where you'll find most of the entertainment as well as some fun little shops.

Arriving at Disney Springs

- *Bus.* All of the resorts have buses to take you to Disney Springs.
- *Boats.* From either of the two Port Orleans resorts you can take a boat to Disney Springs.
- *Walking.* You can walk to Disney Springs from the Saratoga Springs resort.
- *Car.* All parking is free, and the two new parking garages offer handicapped parking.

Wheelchairs, ECVs, and strollers are available to rent at the Sundries location near the Town Center bus loop.

CHAPTER EIGHTEEN

More Magic

For many families, it just hasn't been a vacation without mini golf. Disney has two different courses available. In addition to mini golf, Disney has hosted PGA, LPGA, and USGA events on their four impeccable full-size courses. If you would like to get in a game (or a few) call 407 939-4653 to make reservations. All green fees include a cart. Carts are equipped with GPS to show you the holes and what hazards lie ahead, a small cooler, covers in case of rain, and other necessities.

Note that the two mini-golf courses can be hard to get to if you don't have a car. During the day you can take a bus to Blizzard Beach and Winter Summertime is right there. However, Blizzard Beach is closed at night, so there are no buses. Fantasia Gardens isn't near a bus stop, so if you aren't near the Swan or Dolphin, it's tough to reach. Consider Uber.

Fantasia Gardens

Every hole has a little touch of Sorcerer Mickey's magic, including music, lights, and at one hole Chernabog even makes an appearance. There are sweet scenes with dancing hippos and mushrooms, and then the real magic. My limited experience leads me to believe Disney has designed these holes to help the golfing challenged. We finish Disney mini golf much more quickly than other courses around the country, even though this course is 18 holes. .But they don't take as long, making everyone feel successful and happy.

Sensory Impact. As you enter the cave it could be a little scary, but it really isn't intense.

Winter Summertime Mini Golf

Winter Summertime has two courses to choose from (both 18 holes): one is winter, the other is summer, and both have silly puns and decorations that make kids and adults giggle. This course is also built under trees, so if you are there during the day you will appreciate the shade.

Sensory Impact. No worries!

Everything Else

Here's a sampling of all the *other stuff* there is to do at Disney World:

Spas. Sometimes you need a little attention to your muscles after a long day at the park. There are full-service spas at the Grand Floridian and Saratoga Springs. These spas offer manicures, pedicures, and a full menu of massages, facials, and body treatments. There are also spas and salons at the Coronado Springs, BoardWalk Inn, and the Beach and Yacht Clubs.

Horses and Archery. Fort Wilderness offers horseback riding, pony rides, archery, canoeing, and kayaking. You don't have to be staying at the campgrounds to take advantage of these activities.

Tours and Fireworks Cruises. Tours are available to let you see behind the scenes or experience the parks with a tour guide. There are also boat tours that allow you to see the fireworks on a boat instead of in a crowd. The prices range from expensive to very expensive.

APPENDIX

Complete Packing List

No one going to Disney will ever need *all* the stuff on this packing list. Personalize it by crossing out the items unnecessary for your vacation.

Paper Work

Photo ID for all adults and older-looking teens

MagicBands

Hotel confirmation

Rental car information

Cash/Credit cards

Small bills for tipping and tolls

Envelopes for housekeeping tips

Insurance cards

Membership Cards (AARP, AAA, DVC, etc)

Prescriptions

Service dog / emotional support animal papers

MyDisneyExperience app on your phone

Clothing

Shirts

Sweatshirts or sweaters (air conditioning can be cold at Disney)

Shorts

Pants / capris

Underwear / bras

Pajamas

Belts

Good walking shoes or sandals

Socks

Flip-flops

Hair bands, hair accessories

Hats

Jewelry

Watches

Sunglasses / straps

Swimsuits

Cover-ups

Bandanas

Bibs

Work-out clothes

Laundry Supplies

Detergent (I recommend Pods when traveling)

Dryer sheets

Shout sheets (so you can mix colors safely)

Stain remover

Cash for machines (there are usually change machines)

Wrinkle releasing spray

Tide stick

Toiletries

Toothbrush

Toothpaste

Floss

Deodorant

Razors

Shaving cream

Face soap

Moisturizing lotion

Body lotion

Contacts / Glasses

Contact case

Contact solution

Sunscreen

Lip-balm

Make-up

Make-up remover

Nail polish

Nail polish remover

Cotton swabs

Feminine hygiene

Hand washing soap (there's only bar soap in rooms)

Foot spray

Foot powder

Tweezers

Nail clippers

Nail file

Hairbrush / comb

Hair product

Hair spray

Flat iron / curling iron

Perfume

Travel-size Kleenex

Kids shampoo

Kids bath soap / bubble bath

Kids hair brush / comb

Kids hair accessories

Shampoo, conditioner, and a blow dryer are provided in your room, but you may wish to bring your own

First Aid Kit

Prescription Medications

Pain reliever (for adults and kids)

Band-Aids

Neosporin

Moleskin

Scissors

Anti itch cream / spray

Aloe Vera

Antacids

Motion sickness remedies

Sinus /allergy medicine

Cough drops

Eye drops

MiraLax

Supplements

Icepacks and soft cooler for meds

Diapers / pull ups

Wipes

Diaper creams

Testing equipment

Feeding equipment

Corn silk brushes

Extra chewies

Baby Supplies

Bottles

Formula

Baby food

Spoons

Sippy cups

Bibs

Diapers: regular and swim

Diaper bag

Baby wipes

Pacifiers (never too many)

Blankets

Toys

Kid IDs or temporary tattoos

Outlet covers

Disney provides Pack n Play, strollers (for rent), and car seats in the Minnie Vans, though you may wish to bring your own

Everything Else

Alarm clock
Batteries
Camera'
Memory cards
Cell phones
Power strip
Extension cord
iPad
Sound-blocking headphones
Ear buds
Laptop
External battery
C-Pap machine and supplies
Lanyard (if you don't have MagicBands)
Ponchos
Umbrella
Fan / water bottle contraption for cooling off
Garbage bags (if using a mobility device or stroller)
Ziploc bags (gallon and quart sizes)
Bag for in the parks
Beach bag
Collapsible cooler
Sewing kit
Nightlight
Sound machine for room
Sewing kit
Safety pins
Eyeglass repair kit
Small scissors
Over-door shoe organizer
Shoebox
Bug spray
Antibacterial hand gel

Wet Wipes

Water bottle

Books / magazines

Kindle

Playing cards

Frisbees

Pool toys like a watering can

Pet bowls for food / water

Harness for service/ emotional support animals

Chargers for your camera, phones, tablets, watches, Kindle, external battery wheelchair, oxygen

Disney provides pillows, beach towels, and floaties / life jackets, but you may prefer to bring your own.

Snacks

Gum (it is not sold on Disney property)

Bottled water

Paper plates

Napkins

Pop Tarts

Muffins

Fruit

Peanut butter

Plastic utensils

Special eating utensils

Knife (for cutting fruit)

Cups with lids and straws (to take to Animal Kingdom)

Fruit snacks and other in-park snack items

For the Car (if you're driving)

Paper towels

Wipes

Snacks

Drinks

Small games

Medications

Diapers
Change of clothes for kids
Socks (for stops at indoor playgrounds)
Sunglasses for everyone
Wallet
MagicBands
Book
Phone
Car charger for phones and portable games
Kleenex
Pain reliever
Insurance cards
GPS
Trash bags
Movies
Portable DVD or tablet with movies downloaded
Sound-proof headphones
Pillows
Blankets
Book lights
Ziploc bags (large size in case of motion sickness)

For the Plane (carry-ons)

Photo ID
Wallet with credit cards, cash, and small tipping money
Sound-reducing headphones
MagicBands
Paperwork for service / emotional support animals
Phone
iPad or other tablet with movies downloaded
Car buds
External battery (charged)
Empty sippy cups (fill them on the plane with drinks you purchased)
Empty bottles

Formula
Buy a bottle of water after security
Baby food (check TSA requirements)
Spoon
Diapers
Wipes
Medications
Gum
Chewy candy like Gummi Bears (in case it works better than gum)
Small snacks
Chewie
Bib or bandana
Travel-sized sunscreen
Sunglasses
Books
Small toys (new ones for more interest)
Coloring books
Colored pencils
Pain reliever
Children's pain reliever
Ziploc bags (large size for motion sickness)
Pacifier
Small blanket
Sweatshirts (it can be cold on planes)
Booster seat
Car seat
Water / food dish for service animal
Swim suit if landing before your room will be available
Swim diapers

For the Park

MagicBands
Phone
Phone charger

External battery

Camera (with memory card and charged battery in it)

Snacks

Bottles of water

Sippy cups

Cups with lids and straws (for Animal Kingdom)

Diaper bag with regular supplies

Extra pacifiers

Fan

Ponchos

Extra change of clothes

iPad or other tablet

Charger

Water / food dish for service animal

Paperwork for service animal

Medications and medical supplies

Special eating utensils

Ziploc bags

Sensory Tip: Kids can pack a backpack, too, and a stuffed backpack is often comforting.

Acknowledgments

This book has been a labor of love, and it has taken a village to get it delivered to all of you.

My family—husband Steve, children Ben and Meg—have been completely supportive. They held down the fort when I went to WDW without them (sometimes during a cold Cincinnati winter) and they were always (ok, almost always) open to being guinea pigs. Encouraging me to see this through took patience and pride in me. I can't thank you all enough.

My parents—Jack and Mary Anne Elsener—took me to Disneyland when I was 4 months old. Clearly something stuck! While other families were watching *60 Minutes*, we were watching *Wonderful World of Disney* and *The Muppet Show*. Thank you for teaching me to love most things Disney and more importantly for instilling in me a sense of service. You have both volunteered and been involved in helping others. My wish to see every family live their best lives and have family memories like ours is what drove me to see this book come to light. Thank you!

Debbie Eaton, my traveling partner and sounding board. Thanks for jumping in with me. I got it done, and I have a wonderful friendship that I treasure.

The villagers. There are many that I want to thank for contributions large and small: Emily Duguay, Nathan Elsener, Kim Elsener, Dylan Duguay, Spencer Duguay, Casey Duguay, Charles Elsener, Simon Elsener, Brian Duguay, Dustin Verdin, Len Testa, Jim Hill, Pam Perrino, Kevin Eaton, Phil Eaton, Michelle Porter, Lesley and Tim Sawhook, and Bob McLain. Ya'll know what you did. Thank you!

About the Author

I live in Cincinnati with my husband, Steve, and our two amazing teens. Ben is 20 and has Autism Spectrum Disorder (ASD). Our daughter, Meg, is 18 and typically developing. Raising Ben presented an unexpected journey in life. As I was learning how to give Ben his best start, I found myself advocating for many people with different needs in life. I was answering emails and phone calls almost daily about school choices, summer routines, and very often, how we managed to vacation at Walt Disney World.

I'm currently the chair of the Autism Speaks Cincinnati market and a committee member for "diversity for all abilities in the work force" through the Cincinnati Chamber of Commerce. These commitments allow me to spread awareness and understanding of people with autism and other disabilities.

In my life before children, I grew up in a military family, spent most of my childhood in the Destin, Florida, area where my dad was stationed. I majored in social work at Thomas More College in Crestview Hills Kentucky (a Cincinnati suburb)—and yes, that is where I met Steve.

I have always loved Disney, and worked for them at the Disney Store in Cincinnati.

Now, because every child shapes your path, I'm also becoming a track and cross-country fan. Meg is a NCAA cross-country and track athlete,, so I'm often seen at the track, cheering with my eyes closed.

About Theme Park Press

Theme Park Press publishes books primarily about the Disney company, its history, culture, films, animation, and theme parks, as well as theme parks in general.

Our authors include noted historians, animators, Imagineers, and experts in the theme park industry.

We also publish many books by first-time authors, with topics ranging from fiction to theme park guides.

And we're always looking for new talent. If you'd like to write for us, or if you're interested in the many other titles in our catalog, please visit:

www.ThemeParkPress.com

Theme Park Press Newsletter

Subscribe to our free email newsletter and enjoy:

- Free book downloads and giveaways
- Access to excerpts from our many books
- Announcements of forthcoming releases
- Exclusive additional content and chapters
- And more good stuff available nowhere else

To subscribe, visit www.ThemeParkPress.com, or send email to newsletter@themeparkpress.com.

the easy
guide
to your
Walt Disney World
visit
2018
From the creators of the popular websites
yourfirstvisit.net & easywdw.com
DAVE SHUTE & JOSH HUMPHREY

2018
WALT
DISNEY
WORLD
DINING
GUIDE
Andrea McGann Keech

DISNEY
DEMYSTIFIED
THE STORIES AND SECRETS BEHIND DISNEY'S
FAVORITE THEME PARK ATTRACTIONS
Volume I
DAVID MUMPOWER

SECRET STORIES OF
WALT DISNEY WORLD
Things You Never Knew You Never Knew
JIM KORKIS

Made in the USA
Columbia, SC
27 August 2018